INDIAN PICTURES

DRAWN WITH PEN AND PENCIL

INDIAN PICTURES

DRAWN WITH PEN AND PENCIL

BY THE

REV. W. URWICK, M.A.,

AUTHOR OF "INCIDENTS OF A JOURNEY ROUND THE WORLD," ETC.

GYAN

Published by

Gyan Publishing House
5, Ansari Road
Daryaganj, New Delhi-110002
Phone: 011-47034999, 9811692060
E-mail: books@gyanbooks.com

Distribution Network
gyanbooks.com
India, USA, Canada, UK, Australia, France

ISBN : 978-81-212-2524-3 (HB)
First Published, 1914

2nd Impression 2021

Printed at: Gyan Press, Delhi.

Indian Pictures
Drawn with Pen and Pencil
Author: Rev. W. Urwick

INDIAN PICTURES,

DRAWN WITH PEN AND PENCIL.

BY THE

REV. W. URWICK, M.A.,

AUTHOR OF "INCIDENTS OF A JOURNEY ROUND THE WORLD," ETC.

THE RELIGIOUS TRACT SOCIETY,

56 PATERNOSTER ROW, 65 ST. PAUL'S CHURCHYARD,
AND 164 PICCADILLY.

THE GOLDEN TEMPLE, AMRITSAR.

SNAKE CHARMER.

LONDON: PRINTED BY WILLIAM CLOWES AND SONS, LIMITED.

THE PALACE, LAHORE.

CONTENTS.

CEYLON.

Illustrations.

THE PUNJAB.

Illustrations.

RAJPUTANA AND CENTRAL INDIA AGENCY.

Illustrations.

BOMBAY PRESIDENCY.

Illustrations.

CONTENTS.

MADRAS PRESIDENCY.

THE BENGAL PROVINCES.

THE NORTH-WEST PROVINCES AND OUDE.

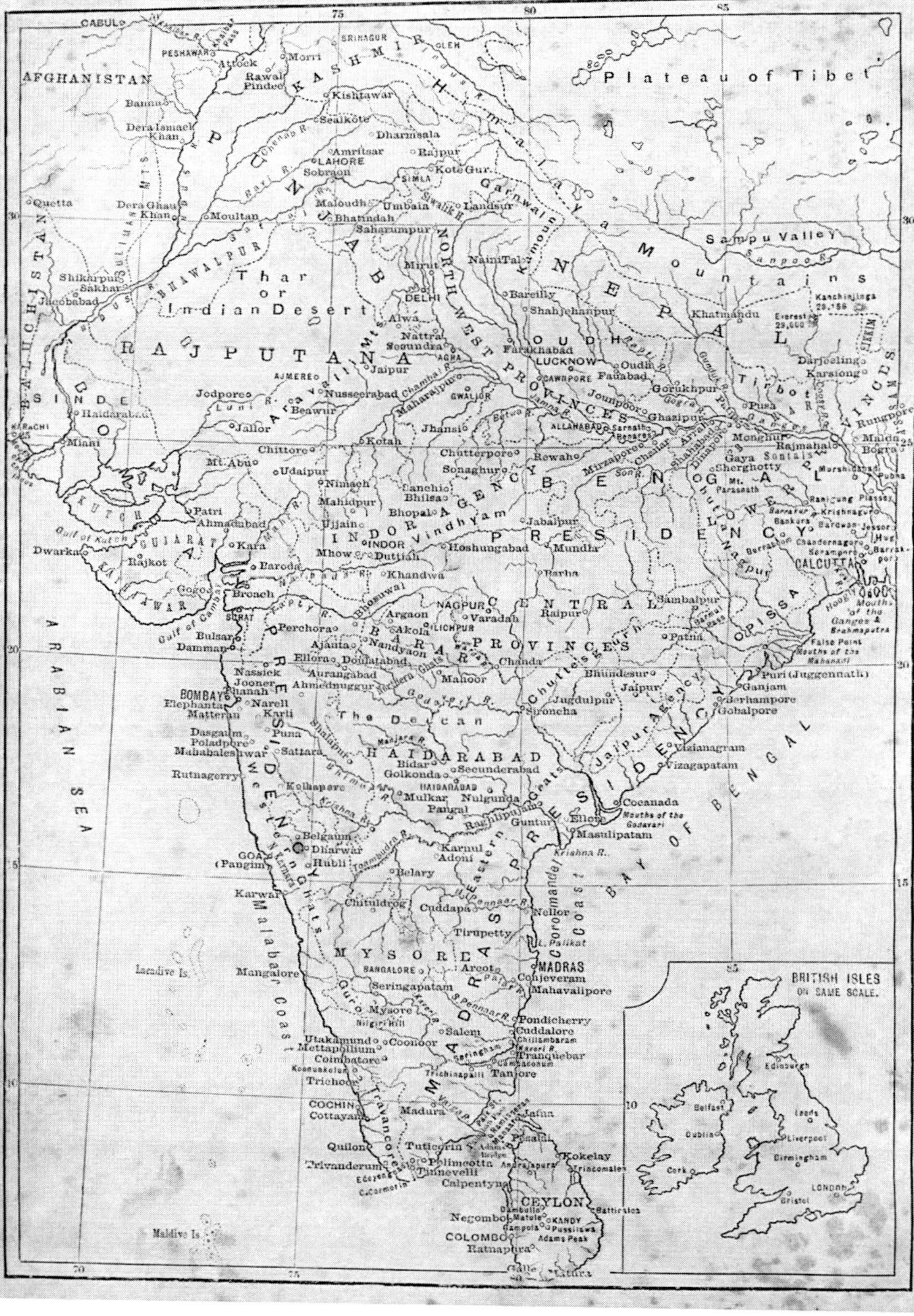
AFGHANISTAN
BALUCHISTAN
KASHMIR
PUNJAB
Plateau of Tibet
Himalaya Mountains
NEPAL
RAJPUTANA
Thar or Indian Desert
SINDE
NORTH WEST PROVINCES
OUDH
INDOR AGENCY
BENGAL PRESIDENCY
LOWER PROVINCES
CENTRAL PROVINCES
BOMBAY PRESIDENCY
HAIDARABAD
The Deccan
MADRAS PRESIDENCY
MYSORE
CEYLON
ARABIAN SEA
BAY OF BENGAL
Malabar Coast
Coromandel Coast
CABUL
PESHAWAR
Attock
Morri
SRINAGUR
LEH
Rawal Pindee
Kishtawar
Bannu
Dera Ismael Khan
Sealkote
Dharmsala
Amritsar
LAHORE
Rajpur
Sobraon
SIMLA
Kote Gur.
Quetta
Dera Ghazi Khan
Moultan
Maloudh
Umbala
Landaur
Bhatindah
Saharunpur
Sampu Valley
Shikarpur
Sakhar
Jacobabad
Mirut
Naini Tal
Bareilly
DELHI
Shahjehanpur
Khatmandu
Everest 29,000
Kanchinjinga
SIKKIM
Alwa
Nattra
Secundra
AGRA
Farakhabad
LUCKNOW
Oudh
Faizabad
Darjeeling
Karsiong
Jaipur
AJMERE
Jodpore
Nusseerabad
Beawur
GWALIOR
CAWNPORE
Gorukhpur
Jounpoor
Ghazipur
Pusa
Rungpore
KARACHI
Haidarabad
Jallor
Jhansi
ALLAHABAD
Benares
Monghir
Rajmahal
Malda
Bogra
Miani
Chittore
Kotah
Chutterpore
Rewah
Mirzaporee
Gaya
Sherghotty
Mt. Parasnath
Mt. Abu
Udaipur
Nimach
Sonaghur
Sanchi
Bhilsa
Mahidpur
Bhopal
Jabalpur
Ranigung
Krishnagur
Bankura
Burdwan
Jessor
Hugli
Chandernagore
Serampore
Barrackpore
KUTCH
Patri
Ahmadabad
Ujjain
Vindhyam
GUJARAT
Gulf of Kutch
Dwarka
Kara
INDOR
Mhow
Duttiah
Hoshungabad
Mundla
CALCUTTA
Rajkot
Baroda
Khandwa
Barha
Gogo
Broach
Bhosawal
NAGPUR
Raipur
Sambalpur
SURAT
Gulf of Cambay
Argaon
Varadah
Mouths of the Ganges & Brahmaputra
Bulsar
Damman
Perchora
Akola
ELICHPUR
Patna
False Point
Mouths of the Mahanadi
Ajanta
Nandyaon
Ellora
Doulatabad
Chanda
Puri (Juggennath)
Nassick
Jooner
Aurangabad
Mahoor
Bhundesur
Jaipur
Ganjam
BOMBAY
Thanah
Ahmednuggur
Elephanta
Narell
Karli
Matteran
Jagdulpur
Sironcha
Berhampore
Gobalpore
Dasgaum
Poladpore
Puna
Mahabaleshwar
Sattara
Bidar
Secunderabad
Vizianagram
Vizagapatam
Rutnagerry
Golkonda
HAIDARABAD
Kolhapore
Mulkar
Nulgunda
Pangul
Cocanada
Mouths of the Godavari
Guntur
Ellore
Masulipatam
Belgaum
Dharwar
GOA (Pangim)
Hubli
Karnul
Adoni
Belary
Karwar
Chituldrog
Cuddapa
Nellor
Tirupetty
Lacadive Is.
Mangalore
BANGALORE
Arcot
MADRAS
Conjeveram
Mahavalipore
Seringapatam
Mysore
Pondicherry
Cuddalore
Salem
Utakamund
Mettapollium
Coonoor
Coimbatore
Tranquebar
Tanjore
Trichinapalli
Trichoor
COCHIN
Cottayam
Madura
Jafna
Quilon
Tuticorin
Trivanderum
Palimcotta
Tinnevelli
Kokelay
Trincomalee
Calpentyn
C. Comorin
Negombo
KANDY
COLOMBO
Adams Peak
Ratnapura
Galle
Maldive Is.
BRITISH ISLES ON SAME SCALE.
Edinburgh
Belfast
Dublin
Leeds
Liverpool
Birmingham
Cork
LONDON
Bristol

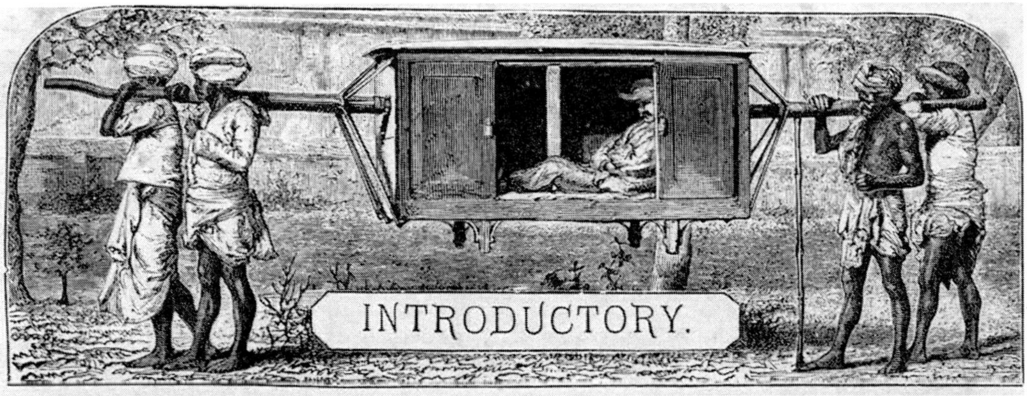

INTRODUCTORY.

INDIA, together with CEYLON, stretches two thousand miles from the Himálayas southwards into the ocean ; and its extreme width, measured across its northern boundary, is nineteen hundred miles. It is as large as Europe less Russia. Physically it divides itself into three parts : (1) the Himâlayas, "the abode of snow," as the name means, where are the treasures of the rain, and the bracing mountain air, forming a double mountain wall against the north ; (2) the River Plains, with the Brahmaputra in the east, the Indus in the west, and the mighty Ganges, "Mother Ganga" adored by the people, across the centre ; (3) the three-sided table land of the Deccan, separated from the river plains by the Vindhya mountains, with the Eastern and Western Ghâts running along either coast and meeting at Cape Comorin. Thus this vast country is naturally isolated, with the sea on either side, the Himâlayan range scimitar-like across the north, its spurs in the east making a natural wall, and the Sulaiman range along the Indus in the west, forming a boundary equally secure.

Of this vast triangle of earth the population is two hundred and forty millions.

As to its Ethnology and Languages we find :

I. The EARLY NON-ARYAN RACES, divided into three great groups : the Thibeto-Burmans, the Kolarians, and the Dravidians.

(*a*) The THIBETO-BURMANS occupy the Himálayas, and include many mountain tribes akin in feature and in tongue to the Chinese.

(*b*) The KOLARIANS, supposed to have come in through the mountain passes, are now scattered on the rugged mountains, in the wide jungles and pathless forests, scattered remains of a primitive population, fierce, black, undersized, muscular, with no written literature—their only monuments stone slabs, flints, and mounds. Of these the chief tribes are the *Sontâls*, and the *Khands.* They were called by their conquerors Dyasus "foes," and Dosas "slaves."

(*c*) The DRAVIDIANS, who also came through the mountain passes, forced their way on in a compact phalanx till they found a secure and permanent resting-place in the south. They attained a high state of civilisation long before the Aryan invasion. Their chief languages, polished and cultivated, are the Telugu—melodious as Italian—the Tamil, rich in its literature, the Canarese, and the Malayalam.

II. The ARYANS, "nobles," as the word means, the wide-spread Indo-European race, whose western branch extends over Greece, Rome, Germany, and England. They, in turn, entered India by the north-west passes, speaking the stately Sanscrit, driving the inferior hordes before them, and finding a permanent home in the great River Plains. The very name of their great works, the Vedas, links them on with ourselves ;—Veda, *οἶδα*, *videre*, *wit* and *wis*dom. They soon asserted their supremacy over the earlier peoples ; as Brahmans and as Rajputs they established Caste, and gave to the East the two giant religious systems of Brahmanism and Buddhism. Their languages were the Sanscrit and Pali, with their branches, Panjabi, Sindhi, Hindi, Bengali, Marhatti and Singalese.

(*a*) *Panjabi* is spoken by the Sikhs, who occupy the northern basin of the Indus, and who were among the first Aryan settlers.

(*b*) *Sindhi* is spoken in the lower valley of the Indus.

(*c*) *Hindi*, which in its purest form closely resembles the parent Sanscrit, and is written in the Nâgari character, is spoken in various dialects in the North-West Provinces.

(*d*) *Bengali* is spoken in the lower valley of the Ganges.

(*e*) *Marhatti* prevails chiefly in the Bombay Presidency. This Hindu race showed its native bravery in the seventeenth century, by overthrowing the Mohammedan power. It was from the Marhattas and the Sikhs as Hindus, and not from the Mohammedans, that we won India.

(*f*) *Singalese* is derived from the *Pali*. *Pali* was the language of Magadha in North India. It was used by the Buddhists and Jains for their sacred books, and it travelled with Buddhism to Ceylon.

The GREEKS invaded India 327 B.C., under Alexander the Great, but left no permanent settlement behind, though the influence of the Greek type of sculpture long survived in Indian art.

SCYTHIC influences and a Scythic era also mark the annals of India from 57 B.C. downwards, and some of the Rajput tribes are traced back to them.

III. The next wave of conquest was that of the MOHAMMEDANS, who entered India in the eleventh century, and made successive conquests. They brought with them their native Arabic; and Arabic inscriptions adorn the magnificent mosques, halls, palaces, and tombs, which they raised chiefly in the seventeenth century. Half the present Mohammedan population in India is Musalman in race.

The religions of India may be classified as follows:

I. BRAHMANISM, the religion of the Aryans, which found its earliest exposition in the hymns of the Vedas, and its development in the institutes of Manu. Originally it was monotheistic. The Rig-Veda, usually placed 1400 years B.C., consists of a series of hymns addressed to bright friendly gods, *devas*, literally, "the shining ones," the great powers of nature, the father-heaven, mother-earth, the encompassing sky. Brahma, the creator, has no separate existence in these hymns. Vishnu, the preserver, is but slightly known, and Siva, the destroyer, appears as Rudra, the god of tempests. The potent prayer was called *Brahma*, and he who offered it *Brahman*. Aleady in the Vedas sacrifices are enjoined, the man-sacrifice, and the great horse-sacrifice of six hundred animals that was substituted for it. And thus by degrees sprang up the four great CASTES: (1) the *Brahmans*, or priests; (2) the *Kshastrias*, or warriors, now called Rajputs; (3) the *Vaisyas*, or husbandmen, and beneath these (4) the servile class, or *Sudras*, "the slaves of black descent." After a long struggle between the priestly and warrior castes, the former prevailed, and established their supremacy as the makers of Sanscrit literature, and the priests and teachers of the people. The Brahman's life was one of discipline. Study occupied his early years; then marriage and family life, next seclusion and devotion, and lastly mendicacy, asceticism, and absorption. Throughout life he practised strict abstinence, recognising the transitory vanity of human life. "What is the world?" says a Brahman sage. "It is even as the bough of a tree on which a bird rests for a night, and in the morning flies away." Self-culture, self-restraint, was the ideal life. Hence, amidst all the changes of history the Brahman in India, refined in features, tall and slim, has calmly ruled.

Brahmanism in its growth and spread strikingly illustrates the teachings of Holy Scripture regarding the gradual lapse of man from a pure and simple faith, from the knowledge of God, into idolatry and superstition. "Knowing God, they glorified Him not as God, but became vain in their imaginations, and their foolish heart was darkened." Brahma the creator became a mere abstract name; Vishnu the preserver received ten incarnations (Avatars) Rama and Krishna being the chief, and Siva the destroyer and reproducer became the embodiment of wrath and lust. The most prominent doctrine of philosophical Brahmanism became the transmigration of souls, ending with absorption into the Supreme Being.

II. BUDDHISM, now the religion, in a degraded form, of one-third of the human race, had its origin in India, whence it has long been exiled. Its founder was Gautăma, son of a prince of the Sakyan clan, born B.C. 623, a hundred miles north of Benares.

After his student and married life, he retired, when thirty years old, to a cave near Gaya, in the Patna district, and this epoch in his life is called "his Great Renunciation." But instead of finding peace in his fasting and seclusion, he reached a crisis of despair, passed through a conflict with the powers of darkness, and emerged with new light and knowledge, to be henceforth know as Buddha, "the Enlightened." This era is known as that of "his Enlightenment." Now he began to live and preach a new life of love and kindness among men, condemning caste, proclaiming the equality of men, and setting before them *Nirvâna*, i.e. cessation, not of existence, but of sin and sorrow, as their final goal. He began this public teaching at the age of thirty-six, and for forty years he laboured. His last words were, "Work out your own salvation with diligence; keep your mind upon my teaching; all things change, but this changes not. I desire to depart; I desire Nirvâna, the eternal rest."

The secret of Gautăma Buddha's success was the truth which his preaching affirmed, viz. (*a*) the overthrow of caste, the equality of Sudra, if just and holy, with Brahman; (*b*) the law of Karma, i.e. conscience or responsibility, that what a man sows he must reap; (*c*) the law of justice and of kindness; and (*d*) Nirvâna, the cessation of all causes of sorrow, to be attained by the practice of virtue. The date of his death is B.C. 543.

Buddhism was a missionary religion, and it spread as a gospel through India. Its Constantine was Asoka, grandson of Chandra Gupta, and King of Maghada (B.C. 250), whose edicts in Pali inscriptions indicate the humanity and kindness of the teaching which the system promulgated. The son of Asoka became Buddhist missionary to Ceylon, and the system spread all over India, as the Topes and Caves of early Buddhism indicate. But it borrowed much from Brahmanism, namely, the doctrine of transmigration, the practice of asceticism, and the recognition of a priestly order. Relics of Buddha were cherished and adored, and shrines built over them. Images of the saint himself were multiplied and became objects of worship. But in process of time Brahmanism in India triumphed over its rival. Buddhism lacked a personal God, it was a form of atheism; it failed to recognize the doctrines of human sin, and of expiation by sacrifice; and here the Brahmins had the advantage, and in time regained their influence and their supremacy. By the tenth century of the Christian era, Buddhism was in India an exiled religion, finding its home in Thibet and Ceylon, in China and Burmah. It has since degenerated into an elaborate Ritualism, akin to Romanism, with the image of Buddha for the crucifix, the goddess of mercy for the Virgin, a shaven, robed and celibate priesthood, altar and lights, the rosary and penance, monks and nuns, purgatory in its series of hells, prayers for the dead, and in Thibet, a pope.

III. HINDUISM is the modern development in India of the religion of the Brahmans, modified by Buddhist teaching. And here again we find only degeneracy from the primitive standards. The Brahmans themselves have in many parts degenerated, and are corpulent, self-indulgent, immoral, worldly-minded men. Caste in all its tyranny prevails. Woman is immured in ignorance, and doomed to slavery. Married when a child, if the child-husband dies, she is a widow for life, doomed to drudgery and neglect. The temples are adorned with revolting and obscene sculptures and frescoes. The images of idolatry are hideous, the objects of adoration countless. VISHNUVISM, or the worship of Vishnu the preserver, and his many incarnations, and SAIVISM, or the worship of Siva the destroyer, form in the present day the very heart and soul of Hinduism. The old idolatry of serpents, trees and stones, borrowed, perhaps, from the non-Aryan tribes, has been adopted into the system, and the Linga bedaubed with red ochre is the popular idol. The *Puranas* are the writings that form the basis of modern Hinduism, and they disclose Phallic worship in all its loathsomeness. The chief daily ceremony in all temples, after washing and dressing the idol, and burning lights and incense before it, consists in offering it food of some kind,—boiled rice, grain, sweetmeats, fruits,—and decorating it with flowers. The smallest village has its own peculiar symbols of worship, rough idols and mere blocks of stone or wood, consecrated to local deities by patches of red paint.

IV. MOHAMMEDANISM appeared in India, first, about the eleventh century, and gained a permanent footing by the conquests of the Moguls. In the seventeenth century its sway was universal in North India. It proclaimed the doctrine, "there is one God, and Mohammed is His prophet," and it built its giant mosques in the great cities. It made many converts; and the Mohammedan population now numbers forty-one millions. But it is a religion, not of love, but of selfishness, lust, and hatred. Most of the Indian Mohammedans are of the Sunni sect. They neither eat nor intermarry with Hindus. Butchers, cooks, and table-servants are for the most part Mohammedans, these occupations being unlawful religiously for the Hindus. *Dhirzis*, or tailors, are Musalmans, and most grooms (*syces*), and coachmen, *Dhobis*, or washermen, *bhistis*, or watercarriers, and *bearers* or house servants are Hindus. The Mohammedans of India ill brook our supremacy. They are ambitious alike of learning and of power.

V. The JAINS are a small sect, but very old, akin to the Buddhists, but having an independent origin. They are a wealthy community, distinguished by the beauty and costliness of their temples, and the multiplicity of their hospitals, especially those for diseased and decrepit animals; they lay great stress on the doctrine of transmigration of souls, and will sweep the seat on which they would sit, or the path along which they would walk, lest they should unwittingly crush an insect. Their chief distinctive feature is saint worship, and their most important holy places of pilgrimage are Mount Abu in the west, and Parasnath in the east.

VI. The PARSÎS are of Persian origin, and are settled chiefly in Bombay, where they have become wealthy and prosperous. They hold the tenets of Zoroaster, and worship the four elements, fire, air, earth and water. The supreme being, called Ormazd, is with them not self-existent, but derived, and they are polytheists in the most rigid sense of the term. They wear a peculiar head-dress, somewhat like a mitre; their scriptures are the Zendavesta; their tongue is akin to Arabic, but they speak English.

To this brief epitome of the races, languages and religions, that from time to time have taken root in India, there remain to be added the settlements of the PORTUGUESE and FRENCH in the sixteenth century, on the east and west coasts, and the settlements and conquests of BRITAIN, consummating in the establishment of her direct rule over one hundred and eighty-six millions of the population, and her protectorate over feudatory states numbering fifty-four millions of souls. Side by side with British conquest, CHRISTIAN MISSIONS have advanced, at first discountenanced, but afterwards protected and encouraged, carrying the truth as it is in JESUS into the cities and villages of the land, unfurling the banner of the Cross amidst the teeming populations, and bringing in its train the civilising and elevating influences of education, science and inventions. Britain has done much for India; there still remains much to be done. Forty millions of our fellow subjects go through life on insufficient food. The food supply must be adjusted by equal land laws to the growing population, and Government expenses must be brought down to the level of a just and bearable taxation. Two hundred millions are the votaries of a debasing idolatry. Christianity and Education hand in hand must accomplish their work of enlightenment for women as well as for men throughout the land.

The order of places in this work follows the route of my journey, beginning with Point de Galle and ending with Bombay. I am indebted to many tourists like myself who have given their impressions to the world for descriptions of scenes which I was unable to visit. For the general subject there are no writers to whom I owe more than to Dr. JAMES FERGUSSON, the great authority on Indian Architecture, and to Dr. W. W. HUNTER, India's ablest statistician. Dr. Hunter's writings have been of invaluable service to me; they stand pre-eminent alike for accuracy of detail, and largeness, breadth, and magnanimity of judgment. The valuable *Manual* of ROPER LETHBRIDGE, Esq., has also been helpful to me. With reference to Ceylon, I am specially indebted to J. W. RHYS DAVIDS, Esq., the Hibbert Lecturer. I beg further to acknowledge the assistance rendered me by RICHARD GARNETT, Esq., of the British Museum Library, GEORGE LOCH, Esq., of the India Civil Service, and Dr. ROST of the India Office. At the suggestion of Sir J. RISDON BENNETT, M.D., I have prefixed this short INTRODUCTION on Indian Ethnology, Languages, and Religions.

CEYLON.

THUPARAMA DAGOBA, ANURAJAPURA.

See Page 33.

COTTAGES NEAR GALLE.

CEYLON.

POSITION AND ASPECT OF THE ISLAND—GALLE AND COLOMBO—NEWERA ELLIA AND PEDRO-TALLA-GALLA—ADAM'S PEAK AND KANDY—THE BO TREE—THE RUINED CITIES, ANURAJAPURA AND POLLONARUA—CHRISTIANITY IN THE ISLAND.

CEYLON in shape and position hangs like a pear from the south-east coast of the Indian Peninsula. The isthmus called Adam's Bridge forms as it were the stalk connecting the island with the continent; the name Adam's Bridge arising from the Mohammedan legend that on his expulsion from Paradise Adam passed by this singular causeway into Ceylon. The isthmus connects Ramisseram with Manaar, and is cut in one place only by a channel called the Paumbam Passage, through which vessels drawing ten feet may pass; but larger ships and steamers to and from Madras and Bombay must go all the way round Ceylon. The northern portion, answering to the thin part of the pear, is one vast forest—interminable jungle—dotted sparsely with specks of yellow green cultivation, but containing the ruins of the two ancient capitals, and on the east coast, the port of Trincomalee. The lower half of the island swells out in the Kandyan provinces into a mass of gneiss and granite mountains, with a margin of rich and luxuriant lower land; and here we find the best scenery, and the chief centres of modern enterprise. Almost in the middle of the island is the capital Kandy, connected by railway with Colombo on the west coast; and at the south-west corner is the ancient and well-known port of call, Point de Galle.

To the sea-trained eye of the voyager across the hot Indian Ocean from the east or west, Ceylon unfolds a scene of loveliness and grandeur unsurpassed by any land. It enjoys two monsoons in the year, and the abundant supply of moisture thus afforded, clothes it with perpetual green. Its slopes are enamelled with verdure; flowers of gorgeous hues deck its plains, palms of all descriptions abound, climbing plants rooted in the rocks hang down in huge festoons, and trees dip their foliage into the sea. By the Brahmans the island was called Lanka, "the resplendent;" by the Buddhists "a pearl upon the brow of India;" by the Chinese "the island of jewels;" by the Greeks "the land of the hyacinth and the ruby." It has with reason been regarded as the country whither the ships of Solomon came for "gold and silver, ivory, and apes, and peacocks" (1 Kings x. 11, 22), and "the almug trees, and precious stones in abundance from Ophir," are the most obvious productions of Ceylon. The very terms by which these things are designated in the Hebrew Bible are identical, Sir J. E. Tennent tells us, with the Tamil names by which some of them are still called. Fable contributes to the charm attaching to Ceylon. The tale of Sinbad in the *Arabian Nights* runs that in the Indian Ocean, near a mountainous island of loadstone, the ships fell asunder, and nails, and everything of iron flew to the loadstone; and hence native boats are put together without the use of iron nails. The "spicy breezes" of poetry, moreover, though hardly in keeping with fact, because the cinnamon gives forth its odour only when crushed, yet bear

SINGALESE MEN OF THE COAST.

witness to the same fascinating charm belonging to the island, and Milton has immortalised them in his great epic where he says:

> "To those who sail
> Beyond the Cape of Hope, and now are past
> Mozambic, off at sea north-east winds blow
> Sabean odours from the spicy shore
> Of Araby the blest."

Ceylon is a little smaller than Ireland, and its population now is two millions and a half. They are mainly of two races, the Tamils, of black complexion and slight-limbed, active and wiry, a mixed Dravidian race from South India, and the Singalese. The Singalese, again, are of two types, the Kandyan type or highlanders, of robust frame, hairy chest, open countenance, yellow brown tint, and the coast Singalese, effeminate-looking, with little beard and long hair rolled into a lump at the back of the head and fastened by a tortoiseshell comb. The Tamils of the north are in religion Brahmans, the Singalese of the south are Buddhists. Buddhism was brought hither from India fully two centuries B.C. Its sacred books in Pali, written on *Olas*, *i.e.* Palmyra palm leaves, are called the *Pitakas*, the three baskets, treasuries, or collections, viz.: 1, Rules of the Order; 2, Doctrine; 3, Supplementary matter. Its temples are called *Dagăbas*. A dagoba—from *dhatu*, a relic, and *gabbhan*, a shrine—is properly a monument raised to preserve one of the relics of Gautăma Buddha. Fragments of his bones, locks of his hair, are inclosed in masses of masonry; a dome of brickwork resting on a square elevated platform covers the shrine, and is surmounted by a *tee* or pinnacle. The oldest of these shrines is that raised by King Tissa, B.C. 200, over the collar-bone of Buddha. The Dagoba of Anurajapura, built B.C. 89, was four hundred feet high—forty feet higher than St. Paul's. Besides Buddhism in the south, and Brahmanism chiefly in the north, there is Mohammedanism among the Moormen, who are in the main of Persian origin. Romanism, planted by the Portuguese,

SINGALESE WOMEN OF THE COAST.

took its complexion from Buddhism, and in its rites conformed to the heathen customs of the people; indeed, the churches at Jaffna, in the north, were fitted up as theatres. The Parawas, or fishermen class, were the first to embrace Christianity.

The *Dipawansa*, "island history," and the *Mahawansa*, "great history," contain the Chronicles of Ceylon. They tell us that for four hundred years, from the seventh to the eleventh century, the incursions and exploits of the Malabars harassed the island. What tended to civilise—as the huge reservoirs called "consecrated lakes" to water the paddy or rice lands still bear witness—was introduced by the northern rulers; and all that contributed to debase is traceable to the Malabars. The reign of Prakrama Bahu, A.D. 1150, stands out prominently as a time of prosperity and advance. Religion and agriculture went hand in hand, and huge tanks were constructed, called "seas of Prakram;" security of life and property was established, so that a girl decked with gold might traverse the island in safety. But it came to pass that in the year 1505 ships from Portugal arrived at Jaffna and Colombo. The Portuguese by degrees gained a footing along the coast, and they held territory there for a hundred and forty years. In 1602 the Dutch began to come, and by degrees overthrew and supplanted the Portuguese, occupying Galle in 1640.

MOORMEN HAWKERS.

Theirs was a military tenure, and lasted also one hundred and forty years. In 1796 their settlements were in turn ceded to the British, who have borne rule ever since, and in 1815 won by conquest the Kandyan provinces.

Nearing Galle, but still some miles from land, we met several of the curiously constructed "double canoes" which the Singalese fishermen use. They are from twenty to thirty feet long, only twenty inches wide, three feet in depth, including the washboard, which is sewn to the gunwale, and are hollowed out of a single stem. The most striking feature about them is the balance-log, a solid buoyant outrigger the same length as the boat,

ON THE ROAD FROM GALLE TO COLOMBO.

and like a second canoe, fixed by two long curved bamboo poles projecting eighteen feet from one side and carrying a high sail hoisted on two poles. This outrigger is always kept to windward when sailing, the canoes having prows at both ends, and being steered with short flat paddles. In these boats the fishermen can sail ten knots an hour, and they venture out twenty miles to sea.

Conveyed from the steamer across the harbour within the old Dutch ramparts, the traveller soon finds himself in Galle, besieged by hawkers (chiefly Moormen) of precious stones, tortoiseshell, ebony, stuffs, and fancy work in wood and gold; but ridding himself of these he will gladly enjoy a stroll along the ramparts and by the lighthouse, and a drive to the Cinnamon Gardens and Wakwella. The cinnamon laurel grows to the height of six or eight feet, and is not barked before the ninth year. Peeling the bark begins in May and lasts till November, but the gardens about Galle and Colombo planted by the Dutch are in melancholy decay, and the beautiful shrubs are growing wild, the cinnamon trade having long ago passed to other lands through the monopoly of the Dutch. Wakwella Bungalow is a lovely spot commanding a fine view of the inland mountains and forests. The roads thither are of a rich red colour, owing to the iron ore or brick-like rock called *Laterite*, and are draped on either side with lovely flowering creepers and shaded with rich foliage.

As we returned we stopped at the foot of a wooded hill, to visit a Buddhist temple, apparently modern and but lately decorated in a very gaudy fashion. The paintings represented scenes in the history of kings and others. Within was a gigantic figure of Buddha, with images of Siva and Vishnu on either side. The Buddhist priests wore bright yellow garments hung on their dark lanky forms. The usual worship consists mainly in the offering of flowers and fruits.

The railway from Galle to Colombo not being yet complete, we drove in her Majesty's mail—a wretched conveyance shockingly horsed—along the lovely road of seventy miles which skirts the shore. It is an avenue of stately palms with a rich undergrowth of tropical trees and gorgeous orchids. Away on the right are the mountains, away to the left glitters the blue sea; the beach is fringed with verdure, and at the headlands the ripples kiss the overhanging leaves. The tides about Ceylon are very slight, the water falling only thirty inches. The white cottages of the natives, each with its garden of cocoa-nuts, nestle in the groves, and the fishermen's canoes skim along the sea. The natives whom we pass look clean and picturesque, but their mouths are invariably discoloured with betel chewing. The leaves of the betel vine together with lime and the sliced nuts of the areca-palm form a tonic, which from time immemorial it has been the national habit to chew, and the mixture imparts a blood-like colour to the mouth. The betel is an intoxicating kind of pepper, and with the

Singalese answers to the opium of the Chinese, and to the tobacco of other nations, but it is not considered so injurious.

COCOA-NUT TREES AND CLIMBERS.

The cocoa-nut trees about the dwellings of the natives along this road are countless; and they have a saying that the cocoa-nut, like the magpie and robin, will only flourish within the sound of the human voice. Like the Palmyra palm in the north of Ceylon, the cocoa-nut in the south yields most of the necessaries of life. Its fruit furnishes food, its shell drinking vessels, its juice palm wine and sugar, its stem materials for building, its leaves roofs, matting, baskets, and paper. The number of these trees in the island is estimated to be twenty millions. The natives climb them with great agility, partly with the help of bamboo ladders, and oftener with the help of a short band of cocoa-nut fibre between the feet or round the loins.

The city of Colombo, whose population now numbers one hundred and twenty thousand, presents but few features of interest to the tourist. It extends about four miles along the coast and two miles inland, and is divided, like most Indian cities, into the black, or native town, and the European quarter. The buildings in the latter are chiefly of Dutch origin—as the fort, the belfry and clock tower, the barracks, and the Wolfendahl Church. The old name Kalambu was altered by the Portuguese to Colombo in honour of Columbus. Here one sees the Singalese chiefly as servants, the Parsees as merchants, the Tamils as labourers, the Moors as retail dealers. The heat at mid-day is most oppressive, but the drive along the Galle Face by the sea at sunset is cool and refreshing. A favourite resort, seven miles south by railway, is Mount Lavinia, on the sea, once a Governor's house, now a hotel, near which is a magnificent banyan tree. In Colombo there are two cathedrals, one Roman Catholic, the other English; and in the street of the dealers in rice is a grotesquely-ornamented Hindoo temple. In Colombo the raw coffee brought from the plantations undergoes the process of curing at several mills for the purpose. Here may be seen, first, the drying of the beans; secondly, the removal of the skin by passing the beans under rollers; thirdly, the picking out of the bad berries, done by women and children; fourthly, the distribution of the different sizes by means of sieves; fifthly, the process

BUDDHIST PRIEST WITH NOVICES.

of packing in huge barrels for exportation. Tamil women are largely employed in these establishments, and present a neat, healthy, and happy appearance. We found the new Museum in the midst of the Cinnamon gardens well worth a visit. Besides the natural and manufactured products of the island, there are here several interesting archæological remains brought from the ruined cities, and in particular a magnificent stone lion. The drive round the lake is lovely, and several miles in extent, but the moist heat was like a perpetual Turkish bath.

The distance from Colombo inland to Kandy is seventy-five miles, and the railway winds its way among the mountains, through scenery combining Alpine grandeur with tropical luxuriance. A huge, isolated hill, called the Bible Rock, from its resemblance to a Bible open upon a cushion, stands out conspicuously in the distance on the right. The line winds and curves round beetling cliffs and overhanging precipices draped with luxuriant creepers. Coolies, *i.e.*, labourers (chiefly Tamils) are conveyed in gangs of not less than six at reduced rates, upon the certificate from their importer or estate manager, and children *under four feet in height* are charged half-fare. The journey occupies four hours and a half. A branch line leads to Gampola, which is the station for Newera Ellia. Gampola, the last of the native capitals, was fifty years ago the cradle, and is still the gateway, of the great coffee plantations. Though the plant had before been brought to Ceylon, the Portuguese and Dutch did little or nothing for its cultivation, and it was not until 1825, that by the removal of the heavy duty the plant rose to importance among the products of the island. Now, all round Gampola, for miles, the hills are covered with coffee plantations. The leaves are bright and smooth, like the laurel, but darker; the flowers are white, and of sweet odour, the berries are crimson like cherries. It is calculated that two hundred thousand natives (chiefly Tamils) are employed on the plantations, which cover over one hundred thousand acres.

A coach runs daily from Gampola, winding up the mountains through Pussilawa, "valley of flowers," to Ramboddie in four hours, and the views are majestic and charming. In the magnificent glen of Ramboddie we reach a barrier of mountains seemingly impassable. Waterfalls on every hand come tumbling over precipices, and roaring through deep ravines mantled with palms and orchids, yellow gamboge trees, and white-flowered daturas. From this point the road climbs the mountain gorge in terraces, cut in many places out of the rock, through a wild forest to the height of six thousand feet; and from the summit of the pass a view of Newera Ellia is obtained. At this height, the coffee plantations give place to those of tea, lately introduced, and found to grow well at this altitude. Several acres of forest have been cleared for tea plantations. From this point you rapidly descend into the far-famed valley of Newera Ellia; and taking up your quarters at one of the homely and comfortable lodging-houses, after the heat of Colombo and the railway, you now feel cold enough to be glad of a fire.

NEWERA ELLIA, the Buxton of Ceylon, its great sanatorium, whither the jaded European, overdone with the heat of Galle or Colombo, resorts for refreshment and rest, is a wide-spreading valley green and grassy, watered by crystal streams, high up among the mountains at the foot of Pedro-talla-galla, the highest mountain in Ceylon. Here one seems to get into England again; English-looking cottages, with gardens full of English flowers, fruit trees, and vegetables; oaks and firs, green fields and hedges, robins and black-

THE PEDRO-TALLA-GALLA RANGE.

birds, bracing breezes and crisp, frosty nights. The temperature ranges from 36° to 81°, and its average at noon is only 62° in the shade. The roads are good, the walks varied, and the mountains on every side invite to a sturdy climb.

A well-kept bridle-path cut through the forest in zigzags leads to the summit of Pedro-talla-galla, which is eight thousand three hundred and forty feet above the sea, or nine hundred and forty feet higher than Adam's Peak. Here one soon gets into the lonely jungle, where in the early morning nature teems with life and motion, and the air is melodious with the voice of birds. We started at 6 A.M. and reached the top of the mountain in two hours and a half. At the height of about seven thousand five hundred feet we came upon a large antlered elk quietly grazing; he gave a deep bark, and scampered off. The Ceylon elk is a large animal, four feet high, of a dark brown colour, rough mane, heavy antlers, and body five feet long. Almost to the summit there is

WATERFALL OF BADULLA OYA.

brushwood, and the rhododendrons were in full bloom. The morning was beautifully fine, and the prospect was most extensive and delightful. The sea was visible in the distance towards the west and south, Adam's Peak to the west, the hills of Kandy to the north, and those of Badulla to the east. From Newera Ellia to Badulla the road descends three thousand feet in forty miles, and commands splendid views. No scene in nature can be more peaceful and lovely than the valley of the Badulla Oya. At Ella the river forces its way through a wild ravine in a series of falls. There are no lakes, properly speaking, in Ceylon, but from these mountain ranges one sees what look like lakes, the immense tanks, relics

CEYLON ELEPHANTS.

of a former civilisation, formed by means of artificial dams drawn across valleys shut in by hills, and making sheets of water six, eight, or ten miles long, by two or three wide. The embankments are from sixty to seventy feet high, and two hundred feet broad at the base; they consist of earthwork, faced in some cases with stone. The design of these immense reservoirs was to supply water for the paddy lands in the districts lying north of the mountains. Every village northwards was provided with a tank, and canals conveyed the water to the fields. They date from the seventh century downwards.

Descending from Pedro-talla-galla, I came upon the track of a wild elephant. The jungle was freshly trodden down, soil disturbed, and trees uprooted. It is an Eastern saying that the last word can never be said about an elephant. When the British first came elephants were numerous, but now they are rare. Very few Ceylon elephants have tusks. They are smaller than the African; twice the circumference of the foot gives the animal's height, which is usually eight or nine feet. They are said to live seventy years, and it is a trite saying, "A dead elephant is never seen." The elephant has marvellous facility in ascending and descending mountains, the joints of the hind legs bending inwards, and enabling them to kneel like a man, and in this posture to slide down, the fore legs being kept straight out. At the approach of the white man they retire: they possess defective sight, but powerful scent. A story is told of a wild elephant at Goa which had got loose in the market-place, and was destroying all before it, but recognising in the crowd the child of a woman who had been in the habit of feeding him when passing her shop, he took it up in his trunk and carried it safely home. Elephants have been exported from Ceylon to India ever since the First Punic War. Of late their numbers have been considerably reduced. They cannot lift the head above the level of the shoulder, and they show timidity and shyness at the sight of man. They like the mountains and the shady thickets. They go in herds, and a solitary elephant is usually a thief.

The famous Adam's Peak may be ascended either from Newera Ellia or the Maskeliya side, where the climb is comparatively easy, or from Ratnapura, on the south side, which is reached by coach from Colombo. The rocky cone which forms its summit is climbed with the help of chains fastened in the rock. A fearful ladder, forty feet high, lands us on the top, where is a small temple, and beneath a sheltered space beside is the *Sri pada*, or footprint, a natural indentation in the rock, artificially made to assume the shape of a man's left foot, five feet long by two and a half broad. The Brahmans call it the footstep of Siva, the Buddhists that of Buddha, the Chinese that of Fo, *i.e.* Buddha, and afterwards the Mohammedans called it the footprint of Adam. Adam, it was fabled, when driven from Paradise took refuge in Ceylon, and spent years of exile on this mountain before his re-union with Eve on Mount Arafath near Mecca. Hence the name Adam's Peak. Between Adam's Peak and the sea quantities of precious stones have been found ; indeed, this is the region where still they are sought—sapphires, amethysts, topazes, rubies. Ratnapura means "the city of rubies," and the sands of the rivers still abound with small particles of tiny gems. Lapidaries use it to polish softer stones. The cat's eye, a green translucent quartz, is specially appreciated by

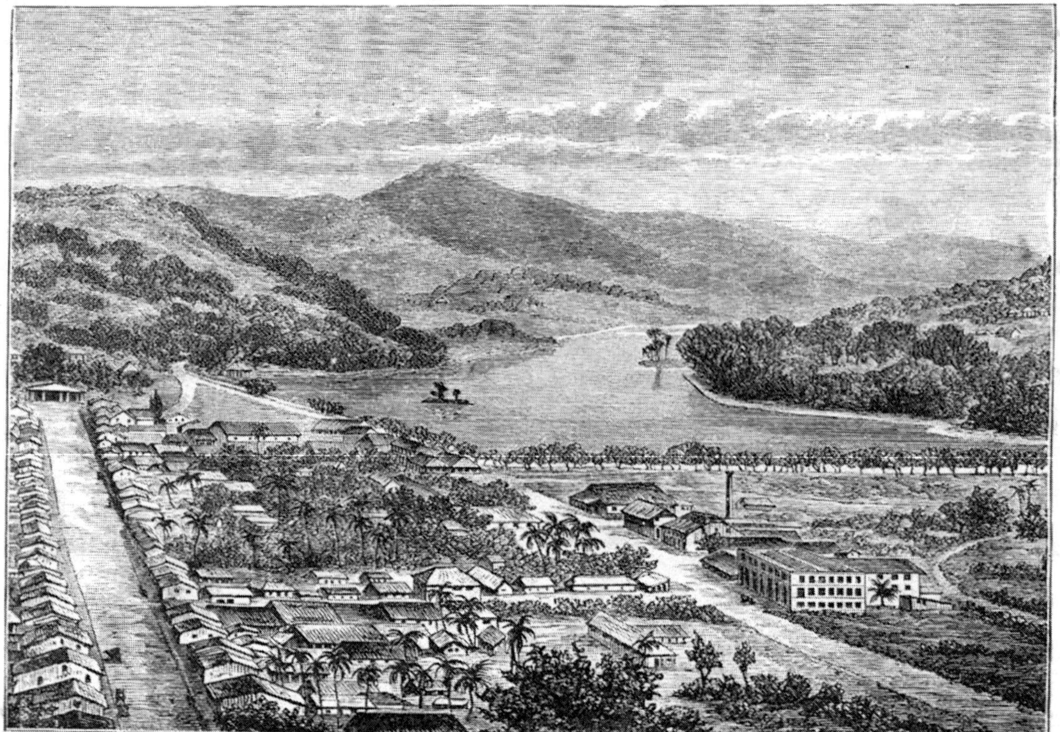

KANDY.

the Singalese. The precarious occupation of gem-hunting is chiefly carried on at Saffragam. The chief polishers and sellers of gems are Moormen.

The tourist in these mountain districts is almost sure to find something he does not want, in the form of leeches, whose presence is first discovered by the chill feeling of the creature hanging heavily on the skin when full and distended. They are about an inch in length, and only one eighth of an inch in thickness, but they swell into more than twice that length and size. They make their way through the finest stocking. They live not in pools, but in rank and damp herbage. In moving, they plant one extremity on the ground and advance by semicircular strides. You may often see them hanging like tassels round the ankles of the palanquin bearers, and dogs and horses are tormented by them. Crocodiles too, are occasionally seen across one's path in dry weather, when the tanks are low, making their way in search of water. They are very tenacious of life, indeed it is almost impossible to kill them.

TEMPLE OF THE DALADA.

Kandy, the ancient capital of the Highland Singalese, is a beautifully situated little city of about ten thousand inhabitants in a nest of hills, itself fifteen hundred feet above the sea; and the thickly wooded hills around it are fully two thousand feet high. At the foot of its main street, which slopes down a hill, is a long artificial lake, made in 1807 by the then King of Kandy; and this sheet of water adds much to the loveliness of the scene. Here, for centuries, the Kandyan kings lived secure, as if in their mountain fastnesses; but upon the conquest of the place by the British in 1815, a road was constructed through the mountains to the coast, which even still presents wonders of engineering skill; and now a railway sends two trains daily to and from Colombo in a four hours' journey. The climate is delightful and the scenery charming. From the fourteenth century downwards, the place has been distinguished as the headquarters of Buddhism, finding its centre in the Temple of the Dalada, the shrine of Buddha's tooth, round which the Buddhist hierarchy gather. This, with the adjoining palace, is the most interesting building in Ceylon. There is an octagonal stone edifice of two stories, in the upper part of which is an Oriental library, containing several valuable Pali manuscripts, and the Buddhist scriptures written on wood and sumptuously bound. A balcony runs outside, on which the kings of Kandy were wont in former times to appear before the people, and to witness performances on the green below.

BUDDHIST TEMPLE, LAKE OF KANDY.

The relic of the left eye-tooth of Gautama Buddha, here said to be enshrined, has a curious history. Rescued from his funeral pile, B.C. 543, it was preserved for eight centuries at Dantapura in South India, and brought to Ceylon A.D. 310. The Malabars afterwards captured it, and took it back to India, but the great Prakrama recovered it. The Portuguese missionaries got possession of it in the sixteenth century, carried it away to Goa, and after refusing a large ransom offered for it by the Singalese, reduced it to powder and destroyed it at Goa in the presence of witnesses. The account of this destruction of the tooth is most circumstantial in the Portuguese records. Nevertheless, the Buddhist priests at Kandy produced another tooth, which they affirmed to be the real relic, that taken by the Portuguese being a counterfeit, and they conducted this to the shrine with great pomp and ceremonial. This is the relic now treasured with such

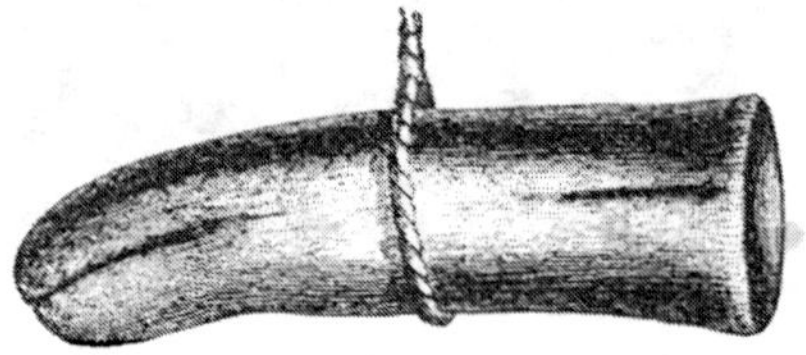

BUDDHA'S TOOTH.

care and reverence. It is probably not a human tooth at all, being, as those who have seen it affirm, much too large (two inches long) ever to have belonged to man. When the British got possession of it in 1815, there was great excitement, the relic being regarded as a sort of national palladium. They allowed it, however, to be restored to its shrine amid great festivities. The sanctuary in which it reposes is a small chamber, without a ray of light, in which the air is stifling, hot and heavy with the perfume of flowers, situated in the inmost recesses of the temple. The frames of the doors of this chamber are inlaid with carved ivory, and on a

SACRED BO TREE, ANURAJAPURA, 2100 YEARS OLD.

massive silver table, three feet six inches high, stands the bell-shaped shrine, jewelled and hung round with chains, and consisting of six cases, the largest five feet high, formed of silver gilt, inlaid with rubies, the others similarly wrought, but diminishing in size gradually, until, on removing the innermost one, about one foot in height, a golden lotus is disclosed, on which reposes the sacred relic. In front of the silver altar is a table upon which worshippers deposit their gifts.

The hills round Kandy command charming views of the city and the outlying district. Gregory's Drive is a new road that winds up the hill above the miniature lake, with bungalows looking out on lovely scenery;

and a path through the opposite woods, called Lady Horton's Walk, leads up to a point commanding a panoramic view of the Vale of Dumbera and the Knuckles range of hills, the river Mahawelli-ganga flowing rapidly below. The Peridenia Botanical garden, covering one hundred and fifty acres, is about three miles from the town, and is rich in all varieties of palms and other tropical plants. A fine avenue of indiarubber trees leads to a noble group of palms, the palmyra, the talipat, the areca, the date palm, the cocoa-nut, and so on,—a huge Kew Palm House in the open air, with a river overhung with bamboos flowing through. The sacred *Bo tree* of the Singalese, to which they as Buddhists attach symbolically the same importance as Christians do to the Cross, is found close to every dagoba. Buddha himself is said to have made frequent allusions to the growth of this tree as an emblem of

GATEWAY LEADING TO THE SACRED TREE, ANURAJAPURA.

the rapid propagation of his faith. It differs from the banyan by sending down no roots from its branches, but its heart-shaped leaves are attached to the stem by so slender a stalk that they appear to be ever in motion, and thus, like the leaves of the aspen, of which the cross was thought to be made, whose leaves are said to tremble in recollection of the crucifixion, those of the Bo tree are supposed by the Buddhists to tremble in remembrance of the sacred scene of which they were the witnesses. It was while reclining under the shade of this tree at Budh Gaya in Magadha or Bihar that Gautama received Buddhahood. The first Bo tree in Ceylon is said to have been sent by Asoka, king of Magadha, a branch from the parent-tree at Uruwela, B.C. 245, and to have been planted at the old capital Anurajapura. It is still pointed out as the oldest tree in the world, and is said to be the parent-tree from which all other Bo trees in the island have been propagated. A wall is now built round it, and a flight of stone steps leads to the sacred enclosure. Pilgrims come to visit it from China, and even from Japan. The solitary column on the right marks the place where Elala, a Malabar invader, who reigned with justice and moderation, fell (B.C. 160). It was erected by his rival in admiration of his bravery, and it is still regarded with veneration. Among the neighbouring ruins is a beautifully carved stone of great antiquity, now forming a doorstep, and representing the lotus flower in the centre, a procession of wild animals on the outside, and in the intermediate circle the *hanza*, or sacred goose, an object of veneration formerly in all parts of India.

Pollonarua and Anurajapura, the two ancient and long ruined capitals

CARVED STONE AT ANURAJAPURA.

of Ceylon, lie to the north-east and north of Kandy. The tourist starts by the road to Trincomalee as far as Matale, sixteen miles, near which (three miles off) is a cave temple, called the *Alu Wihare*, curiously built, amid loose and tumbled masses of rock. The place is specially interesting as the spot where, as the Mahawanso says, the books of Buddhism were first compiled, and its precepts reduced to writing. The statement runs: "The wise monks of former days handed down the text of the Three Pitakas by word of mouth. But seeing the destruction of men, the monks of this time assembled, and, that the Faith might last, wrote them in books." Leaving Matale, we make our way through Nalande (fourteen miles) to Dambulla (fifteen miles), where is one of the oldest rock temples in Ceylon. The rock is five hundred feet high, and is visible from afar. The temple is reached by hewn steps, and upon climbing these we behold a noble gateway adorned with carvings. The building was known as "the cave of the golden rock," darkness being the characteristic of the interior of all Buddhist temples. Indeed, the word Wihara or Vihara, now denoting any Buddhist temple or monastery, literally signifies "a residence." In the forest stretching south of Dambulla there stands a colossal statue of Buddha carved in a mass of rock. It is upwards of fifty feet high, and reminds one of the Daibutz of Japan. It would appear that in early times this statue was roofed over. It is called the Aukana Wihara.

The road leads on through jungle by the great tank of Topare to POLLONARUA, or Pulastipura, where are the ruins of a city built by the famous King Prakrama Bahu, which continued to be the capital of the Kandyan

CARVED STONE AT ANURAJAPURA.

monarchs till the fourteenth century. The remains are extensive and interesting, displaying beauty of design and excellence of execution. The forest abounds with them, but perhaps the most striking is the Jayata-wana-rama, a huge Buddhist temple, containing, between two octagonal towers forming the main entrance, a statue of Buddha, fifty feet high, formed of brick covered with polished *chunam* or cement. The side view gives a good idea of the elaborate carving and extensive range of this building.

Another still more curious building at Pulastipura is the Gal-wihara, a rock temple, which has in front four richly-carved columns, a raised altar, with a statue of Buddha seated, a statue of Buddha standing, and a statue of the same famous saint reclining—forty-five feet in length—the attitude of his attaining Nirvana.

North of Matale about sixty miles is another and still more ancient ruined city called ANURAJAPURA. According to the narrative of the Mahawanso this city was founded four hundred years B.C. When King Asoka sent his son Mahinda to introduce Buddhism to Ceylon, the reigning monarch was Tissa (250–230 B.C.) who received him with favour and espoused the new religion. He built the famous temple called the Thuparama Dagoba, of bell-shaped outline, the most elegant in Ceylon, which

JETAWAN-ARAMA DAGOBA.

still rises sixty-three feet from the ground, and stands on a platform fifty yards square, with three rows of monolith pillars twenty-six feet high, one hundred and fifty in all. He erected it as a shrine for the right collar-bone of Buddha. The pillars are supposed to represent and answer to the stone rail surrounding the topes in India. They were probably connected with each other by beams of wood and frames of canvas covered with paintings. Paintings, as distinct from sculptures, are characteristic of Ceylon temples.

A precipitous rocky hill, a thousand feet high, eight miles to the east, connected with the city by a long street, was chosen as an appropriate site for another huge temple of brick, under which was deposited another relic of Buddha—a hair which grew on a mole between his eyebrows. Regarding this hill, the hill of Mihintale, a visitor to it thus writes: "It was on this hill, the three peaks of which, each now surmounted by a dagoba, form so striking an object from the central trunk road which runs along its side, that the famous missionary Mahinda spent most of his after years. Here, on the precipitous western side of the hill, under a large mass of granite rock, at a spot which, completely shut out from the world, affords a magnificent view of the plains below, he had his study hollowed out, and steps cut in the rock over which alone it could be reached. The great rock effectually protects the cave from the heat of the sun, in whose warm light

GAL-WIHARA, PULASTIPURA; IMAGE OF BUDDHA RECUMBENT.

the valley below lies basking; not a sound reaches it from the plain, now a far-reaching forest, then full of busy homesteads; there is only heard that hum of insects which never ceases, and the rustling of the leaves of the trees which cling to the sides of the precipice. I shall not easily forget the day when I first entered that lonely, cool, and quiet chamber, so simple and yet so beautiful, where more than two thousand years ago the great teacher of Ceylon had sat and thought and worked through long years of his peaceful and useful life. On that hill he afterwards died, and his ashes still rest under the dagoba, which is the principal object of the reverence and care of the few monks who still reside in the Mahintale Wihare."[1]

The square of the entire city of Anurajapura, including tanks, was walled

[1] *Buddhism*, by T. W. Rhys Davids. Society for Promoting Christian Knowledge.

in about B.C. 48, by Queen Anula, and each side is said to have been sixteen miles long. The entire distance from Anurajapura to Colombo by way of Kandy is one hundred and sixty miles.

Conjectures have been eagerly made concerning traces of Christianity in Ceylon in the early centuries; but if in those days there were any Christians in Ceylon, they must have been sojourners only from among the Syrian Christians on the Coromandel coast. "Its light appears," says Sir J. E. Tennent, "to have been transiently kindled, and to have speedily

RUANVELLY DAGOBA, ANURAJAPURA.

become extinguished." Cosmas, A.D. 535, speaks of Christians here, with a priest and deacon ordained in Persia. These were probably Nestorians. The two Mohammedan travellers of the ninth century, whose narratives have been translated, are silent as to the existence of any form of Christianity, and Marco Polo, A.D. 1290, declares that the inhabitants were idolaters. The Portuguese in the sixteenth century brought with them Romanism, and Xâvier was invited in 1544 to come to Jaffna, but though many were baptized, he has recorded his disappointment at the inward unsoundness of all he had outwardly achieved. Many natives, both in the north and in the south, became Roman Catholics; but, in the charges officially brought against the Jesuits, it was alleged to be doubtful whether by affecting idolatry, and tolerating it amongst their proselytes, they had not themselves become converts to Hinduism rather than made Hindus converts to Christianity. They assumed the character of Brahmins of a superior caste, and even composed a pretended Veda. They conducted images of the Virgin in triumphal procession, imitated from the orgies of Juggernaut. Among their most distinguished preachers has been Joseph Vaz (died at Kandy, 1711), who added to the Church thirty thousand converts from the heathen. The Dutch on their coming established the Reformed Church of Holland as the religion of the colony, and the first Presbyterian clergyman began his ministrations in 1642. In 1658 they issued a proclamation forbidding the presence of Roman Catholic priests; and finding this to fail, they issued another forbidding them to administer baptism. They pulled down and broke the Romanist images, and in Jaffna took possession of the churches. But, in spite of all this severity, Romanism kept its ground, and the Dutch missionaries did not succeed. Notwithstanding the thousands of Singalese once enrolled as converts, the discipline of the Dutch Presbyterians is now almost extinct among the natives. Baptism with registration was, in fact, regarded as a government qualification, a badge of civil rights, and submitted to as such. Children were brought in crowds, and the ceremony was performed by arranging them in rows and sprinkling their faces with water as the administrator walked along. Cases are on record where the parent, living far from Colombo, borrowed an infant in the town, and had it baptized and registered in the name of the child who was at home. Since the British rule began, this coercive policy has ceased, and the Gospel has been preached in a

MUDALIYAR OR HEADMAN.

Christian spirit. In 1816 Ceylon was made an archdeaconry under the see of Calcutta. It was made a bishopric in 1845. Protestant missions, set on foot by the American Board in 1816, have been uninterruptedly

COLOSSAL IMAGE OF BUDDHA.

efficient. Upwards of six hundred students have been under instruction from time to time in the American seminary at Batticotta; and of these more than half have openly professed Christianity, and all have been more or less imbued with its spirit. The majority are filling situations of credit and responsibility in the island. The Wesleyans also have been and are still extensively at work with churches, colleges, and schools in North and South Ceylon: and the Baptists have useful missions at Ratnapura, at the foot of Adam's Peak and among the pilgrims thither, at Colombo, and at Kandy. Lastly, the Church Missionary Society has been successful in several stations, though of late years unfortunate hindrances have sprung up through Ritualistic tendencies and claims of the newly-appointed bishop. Out of the taxes levied upon the native population the sum of twelve thousand pounds is annually paid by the government in support of this episcopate and other religious establishments in the island. The Kandy Collegiate School educates a large number of boys and young men. Nevertheless, Brahmanism has still a strong hold upon the Tamils of the north, and Buddhism, with its flower-offering and devil-worship, is still vigorous among the Singalese. Books, too, in favour of Buddhism, with extracts from English writers who extol its early literature, are published and circulated. Evangelical Christianity is, however, gaining ground, and the present census will probably show the number of Protestants to be upwards of seventy thousand. A scheme of disendowment is proposed, to take effect in five years.

COCOA-NUT PALMS AND JUNGLE.

GRAND PAGODA, CONJEVERAM; GOPURA AND SACRED TANK.

MADRAS PRESIDENCY.

CHAPEL OF THE SACRED BULL, CHILLAMBARAM.

MADRAS PRESIDENCY.

TINNEVELLY AND TRAVANCORE—THE DRAVIDIAN TEMPLES—MADURA—TRICHINOPOLY —TANJORE—MADRAS—THE COAST VOYAGE NORTHWARDS.

CEYLON is linked on to India not only by a natural isthmus or chain of alternate islands and sandbanks, and politically by a government under the same crown of Britain, but by a continual transfer of population to and from the mainland. The Tamils, who are the chief work-people on the coffee plantations of Ceylon, come from the Madras Presidency, and they do not generally settle permanently in the island. There is a continual stream of comers and goers, and there are six ports on the western coast of Ceylon, to and from which vessels run to the Coromandel Coast, as the eastern side of Southern India is called. Of these six ports the chief are Pesalai and Vankalai in the north, and Colombo on the west. In 1874, for example, there arrived in Ceylon one hundred and twenty-five thousand of these Indian coolies, and the departures numbered ninety thousand. A great exodus always follows the gathering of the crop; in the steamer in which we crossed from Colombo to Tuticorin (one hundred and fifty miles) there were about five hundred Tamils, men, women and children, on board returning to their native land. Many of them crowded the deck all night, and, in spite of much roughness from the sailors and boatmen, seemed patient and light-hearted. The noise and jabbering as the boats conveying them from shore swarmed round the steamer was amusing, and almost deafening. There is certainly no lack of talk, no taciturnity among them. After a calm starlight night we found our vessel anchored off the flat sandy coast of India, about six miles from shore. The steamer could not be brought nearer on account of the shallows; and though the sea was calm the billows of a heavy swell chased each other over the sandbanks with a long lazy sweep, towards the land. A fleet of heavy native sail-boats came out to take the passengers ashore; and in a four-oared boat, after passing Hare Island, we reached the landing-stage of Tuticorin in an hour. Tuticorin was once celebrated for its pearl fishery, and is now a town rising in importance as the terminus of the South Indian Railway. It is the main port of the District of Tinnevelly, a district which, together with the Native State of Travancore, forms the southern part of India. Cape Comorin itself is within the boundary of Travancore, but Tinnevelly occupies two-thirds of the breadth of the peninsula. These two provinces are separated by the range of Western Ghauts, which run north and south along the western coast, rising to the height of seven thousand feet, and are the highest mountains to be met with till we come to the Himálayas. Tinnevelly is about the size of Yorkshire, and has a population of a million and a half. Northwards, the country is well cultivated, and of a green fertile aspect, paddy lands extending for miles on either side the railway; but southwards there stretches a vast sandy plain of a fiery red colour, dotted over by groves of tall majestic Palmyra palms. While all around is parched and arid, this tree strikes its roots forty feet below the surface, gathers up the moisture, and daily gives forth quantities of sap called "toddy," which is collected in small earthen vessels attached to the tree, and is largely manufactured into sugar. The Shanar labourer climbs thirty or forty trees seventy feet high twice every day to collect the sap. The Hindus call the Palmyra "the tree of life," and dedicate it to Ganesh. It gives three quarts of "toddy" daily, its wood is hard and durable, and its leaves thatch the native houses, are woven into mats and baskets, or smoothed by pressure, they serve for books and parchments. In a word, the Palmyra palm in South India as well as in the north-east of Ceylon supplies shelter, furniture, food, drink, oil, and fuel for the people, with forage for their cattle and utensils for their farms.

It is an interesting fact that Tinnevelly and Travancore, more than any

PAGODA, TINNEVELLY.

other part of India, have been brought under the influence of Christianity, and this from the earliest times. The Christians of St. Thomas, as they are called, early in the third century, it is supposed, occupied portions of the Coromandel Coast on the east, and of the Malabar Coast on the west. Indeed, the Syrian Churches here claim to have sprung from the preaching of the Apostle Thomas himself; however this may be, a Syriac MS. of the Bible, brought from this district, now at Cambridge, is said to date from the eighth century. And in modern times Christian missions have been

MAHÉ, MALABAR COAST.

more successful here than anywhere else in India. Travancore, unlike Tinnevelly, is a mountainous country full of diversified scenery. In its northern part, the Malayâlam language is spoken. The view from the Peak of Agastya, seven thousand feet high, which is usually ascended from Trivanderum, is said to be the finest in Southern India. As on the east the Palmyra, so on the west of these mountains the Cocoa-nut palm flourishes. Here there is quite a nest of missions. The population of Travancore numbers upwards of two millions, of whom one-fifth is Christian.

The London Missionary Society takes the lead, and the census report witnesses that "by the indefatigable labours and self-denying earnestness

CHRISTIAN NATIVE GIRLS.

of the learned body of the missionaries in the country, the large community of Native Christians are rapidly advancing in their moral, intellectual and material condition." Travancore is perhaps one of the best governed and most enlightened native states in India. North of it, on the west coast, is Cochin, near to which is the old Hebrew colony known as "the Black Jews of Malabar." Their religious knowledge is much narrower than that of the "White Jews," who have been settled there since the destruction of Jerusalem. The Black Jews are supposed to have come thither upon the conquest of the Ten Tribes, and perhaps through Afghanistan.

Taking the train which runs through Maniachi Junction, a branch line brought us in three hours to Tinnevelly. The railway terminus here is half-way between the town of Tinnevelly and the celebrated settlement of Palimcotta. The River Tambiravarni ("the copper-coloured river") rising in the Ghauts, near the famous Falls of Papanasum, waters the plain and

TAMILS OF SOUTH INDIA.

gives it a most fertile aspect. The country is covered with cotton and rice-fields. Tinnevelly, the native city, with its Temple of Siva, lies to the west, and Palimcotta, fifty-seven miles from Cape Comorin, the English station, to the east. Nothing can be more strange and pleasant to the eye of a Christian than to see the spire of a Christian church, with the surroundings of a missionary compound, rising amid the emblems of decaying heathendom in that far-off land. Hearing the church bell on the quiet Sunday morning, and seeing the schools and the people wending their way to worship, one might almost fancy oneself in some neat English village, were it not for the dark faces of the villagers and the strange tower of an old heathen temple looming above the trees. The mission here was begun by the Danish missionaries in 1771, and Schwartz himself visited Palimcotta twice. The Christians of the district now constitute one-fifth of the population, but they are for the most part from among the lowest castes, *i.e.* the Shanars, the caste of Palmyra-climbers. Two veteran missionaries are at present at the head of Christian effort in the district, namely, Bishop Sargent at Palimcotta, and Bishop Caldwell at Edeyengoody, thirty miles south-east. Large numbers of natives are putting themselves under Christian instruction, in the hope of protection from oppression, for there is much oppression in every Indian village; and by connection with a strong English mission there is hope that they may get their wrongs redressed. Many more have joined the Christians in their gratitude for relief given in time of famine. But, whatever the motive, they hear the Gospel message, and are instructed in Christian truth; they become intelligent, progressive, promising.

The cleverness and intelligence of the natives when well educated is manifest from the following examples which Bishop Sargent gave us. He had at table one day a young native who had passed the Indian Civil Service examination—a gigantic labour and achievement for any man, but especially for a Hindu—and who had thoroughly mastered not only the English language, but our English literature also. To test his memory and his knowledge, each one at table quoted some familiar lines from an English poet; and thereupon the young Tamil not only recited each quotation, but named the work it was from, gave the connection and the author's name. "Your quotation," he began, "was so and so, from such a play of Shakespeare, and this is the connection;" and so on to each one round the table. Again, a native missionary was once asked when preaching, "How do you explain the differences among you? Here are Church Missionary and Propagation Society missionaries, Baptist missionaries, Presbyterian and London Society missionaries. How are we to tell which is right?" The native preacher replied: "There was once a dispute among the fingers of the hand, which should have the pre-eminence. The *thumb* said, 'I ought to have the pre-eminence, for it is plain, you can none of you do anything without me.' 'Ah,' said the *first* finger, 'what is more important than pointing out the way? This is my office; I ought to have the pre-eminence.' 'I,' said the *second* finger, 'rest my claim on mathematical principles. When you hold the hand upright, which finger is the tallest? I am; therefore I ought to have the pre-eminence.' 'No,' said the *third* finger, 'for though it is something to point out the way, and mathematics too are strong, there is one thing stronger, and that is love. And when you put the symbol of love upon the hand it is the third finger that you choose; therefore the supremacy is mine.' 'Hear me too,' said the little finger; 'true, indeed, I am small and you are large, mathematics are strong, and love is stronger, but there is one thing higher than all, and that is worship; and when you approach the god, I am the finger that you choose to present nearest in

PAGODA OF CHILLAMBARAM.

your prayer, for you press your hands together, lift them up, and hold them thus. Therefore I should have the pre-eminence.' Now," continued the

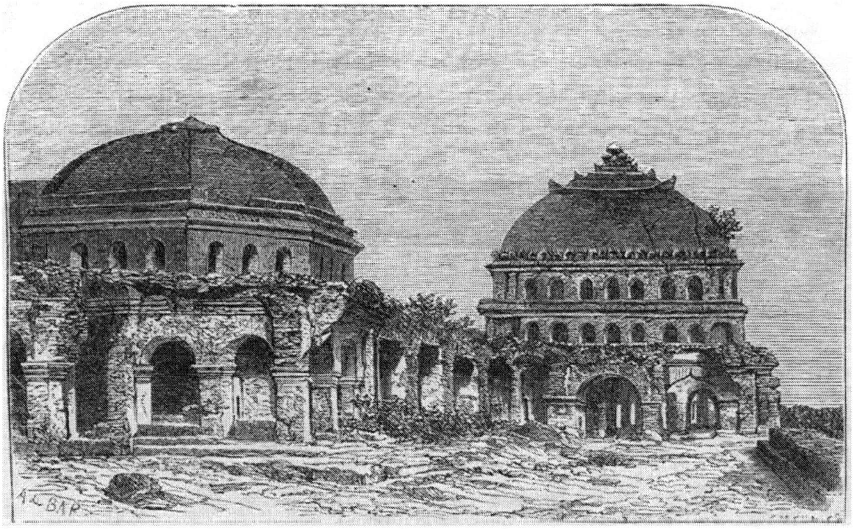

RUINED PERUMAL PAGODA.

native pastor, "each finger has something to say for itself, each is important in its way; and so with the various Christian Societies. But all derive their

GREAT HALL OR AUDIENCE CHAMBER IN THE PALACE OF TIRUMALA, MADURA.

life and strength from a common source, and all working harmoniously under the guidance of a common Will, become mighty for the accomplishment of Christ's work in the world." These two examples show how the Hindu may become fully competent both for the Indian Civil Service and for missionary work in India.

The whole of that part of Southern India that lies between the eighth and the sixteenth parallels of latitude used to be called the Carnatic or Black Country, and is peopled by the Dravidian race. The Dravidians were

TIRUMALA'S CHOULTRY, MADURA.

not the aborigines of the country; they were, like the Aryans of the north, early immigrants who came in successive waves from some part of Central Asia, and settled chiefly in the southern portion of the great peninsula. They are quite distinct from the Aryans; their skin is darker, and their language different. They form one-fifth of the whole population of India. They are active, hard-working, docile and enduring. They are more sober, self-denying, and less brutish in their habits than Europeans. They show greater respect for animal life, they have more natural courtesy of manner, and, as servants, attach themselves to those who treat them well with far greater affection than English servants. The Dravidian tongue embraces four groups of languages, Tamil, Telugu, Canarese, and Malayâlam.

ENTRANCE TO THE PUTHA MANDAPAM, MADURA.

The railway from Tinnevelly runs north, about a hundred miles through a flat productive country, in about seven hours to Madura, the ancient capital of the large district which bears that name. Madura was for centuries before the Mohammedan conquest the metropolis of South Indian learning and religion ; and the ruins of the palace, together with the immense Temple of Siva, covering twenty acres, are standing memorials of its early greatness. Here we come face to face with the masterpieces of Dravidian architecture for which the Madras Presidency is famous, and which in their number, their vastness, and the elaborateness of their workmanship, astonish and almost bewilder the Christian tourist. The Dravidians of Southern India offered their labour to their gods. Their temples are divided into the following parts :—

ENTRANCE TO THE GREAT HALL, PALACE OF TIRUMALA, MADURA.

I. The Vimana or Adytum, square, and surmounted by a pyramidal roof overlaid with gold. Here, in a dark cubical cell, the altar and idol are immured, and a lamp is kept burning dimly night and day.

II. Around the Vimana, and leading up to it usually from the four points of the compass, are the Mantapas, huge stone porches richly carved.

III. The Gopuras, or gate pyramids, the most obvious features from the outside, towering two hundred feet high, and elaborately carved with a congeries of most grotesque figures in stone. They are raised tier upon tier in diminishing stories, of which there are from ten to fourteen, and they terminate in an oblong dome-top.

IV. The pillared halls, or Choultries, commonly from ten to twenty feet high, with a thousand stone pillars elaborately carved from base to capital and shaped into divers figures, and supporting a flat stone roof.

V. Sacred Tanks, surrounded with corridors and with flights of steps descending into the water.

All these, gathered round and leading to a common centre in the adytum, form together the monster wide-spreading temple of South India called the PAGODA.

The Pagoda of Madura has nine towers or gopuras, one of which we ascended by a narrow staircase leading from story to story to the highest, each small chamber with pigeon-holes in its walls, opening north and south: but the peeps thus gained, being very limited, hardly repaid the fatigue of the climb. This temple dates from the third century B.C.; it was destroyed in A.D. 1324, and restored in the seventeenth century. It is kept in good repair, and many masons were still at work upon it. It is dedicated partly to Minakshi, the fish-eyed goddess, and partly to Siva.

Passing through the gopuras and along corridors used as bazaars, we came to the dark flat-roofed choultry, or hall of a thousand pillars, each pillar being of stone, some of black granite, all carved more or less elaborately, and representing male and female deities dancing. One of the figures is said to represent the devil, and boys are allowed to spit in his face. One pillar is subdivided into twenty-four smaller ones. A corridor built by Tirumala, three hundred and thirty feet long, by one hundred and five in width, with stone figures of Yali, a strange monster, the lion of the south, on either side, leads on to the sacred tank—about fifty yards square, and full of dark green water—in which some Brahmans were bathing. The corridors around this tank are covered internally with fresco- paintings, some astronomical, others of a gross character. There are three different statues of the bull sacred to Siva, as the shrine is approached. Admission to the shrine itself is prohibited, and as you look up the aisle within, all is darkness and stillness, save in the distance the glimmer of the lamp before the idol. The favourite idols are plastered with oil and red ochre; and there is a general greasiness about the precincts by no means fragrant or cleanly. Outside the great pagoda, in the street, stands the car in which the idol is taken round the city in pomp on festive occasions. Grandeur and abomination, massiveness and uncleanness are in this temple strangely combined.

Another celebrated building in Madura, now in great part ruined, is the Palace of Tirumala, one of the greatest of the rulers of the province, built by him in 1623. The hall is a quadrangle, two hundred and fifty by one hundred and fifty feet, and with an elaborate corridor, and one hundred and twenty-eight massive granite pillars ornamented with stucco, made from *chunam*, or shell lime, which is a characteristic of the Madras Presidency. The British Government is now restoring it, and using it for legislative purposes.

On the other side of the town there is a lovely drive leading to a large sacred tank, the Teppu-kulam, with an island and temple in the centre. The road is arched over and shaded with banyan trees; and a very fine specimen of this tree is to be seen in the garden of the Collector. The COLLECTOR in India is, of course, the Civil Servant, a prince in his way, who represents government in the District. Under the Collector in a Zillah District there are usually four Assistant Collectors, and on a level with him one District Judge, with two Assistant judges, one Superintendent of Police, with an assistant, and

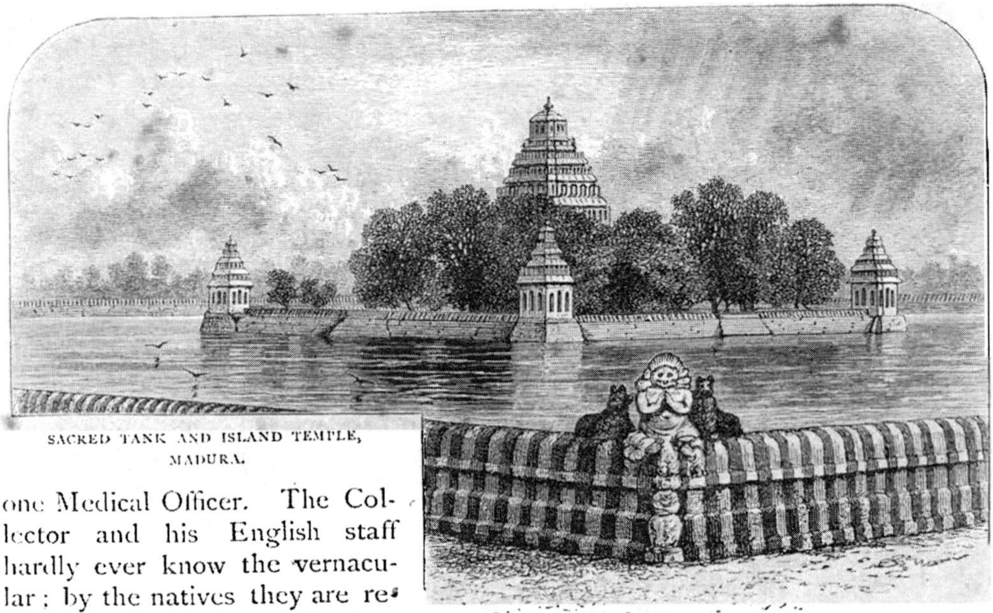

SACRED TANK AND ISLAND TEMPLE, MADURA.

one Medical Officer. The Collector and his English staff hardly ever know the vernacular; by the natives they are regarded with awe, not affection, and too often want of consideration flows from want of intimacy. A Zillah District is in extent somewhat like an English county, and usually contains an area of two or three thousand square miles, and a population of one or two millions. "The Collector is separated by an impassable gulf from the people of the country," says Sir J. B. Phear; and he adds, "to the eyes of a native, the English official is an incomprehensible being, inaccessible, selfish, overbearing, irresistible." This statement is made with reference to the Bengal Presidency, and it applies in its full force to that of Madras. The Collector is paid from the taxes two or three thousand pounds sterling a year, and retires with an annual pension of a thousand pounds.

At Madura the American Board has a very efficient mission, with valuable schools. It was founded in 1834; since which time it has covered the entire province with a network of stations. It includes one hundred and thirty-eight congregations, a hundred native missionaries, and a hundred native teachers. The institution of boarding-schools, peculiar to missions in Southern India, was introduced by the American Board, and there are in the Madura province one hundred and eighteen schools and training colleges.

In India, even in the coolest season, if you want coolness, you must rise early. It was New Year's morning, and the bright stars of the Southern Cross were still shining, when we drove in the missionary's conveyance to the railway station and took the early train one hundred miles northwards for Trichinopoly, a city often taken and retaken in the wars between the French and English in the last century. The sun rose in a clear sky at 6.30, and hills sweeping up from the plain were kindled by his beams. The peasants were already at work like dark skeletons upon the land, employed chiefly in lifting water from wells and tanks by means of long bamboo levers, and pouring it into trenches cut through the rice-fields. Long before we arrived the famous rock of TRICHINOPOLY was in view before us, and we

ROCK AND TEMPLE, TRICHINOPOLY.

reached the city in the heat of the day, after a seven hours' journey.

The main feature of Trichinopoly is its noble rock of syenite, rising abruptly five hundred feet above the sea, and towering two hundred and fifty feet over the town. Half way up is a temple to Siva, cut in the rock and built against it. We climbed stair after stair, and up the last dangerous flight of steps cut in the bare precipitous rock, without banister or rail, to the Mandepam or pavilion on the summit, a temple to the god Ganesh.

Here there presents itself a clear and extensive view in every direction over the wide-spreading plain, northwards over Seringham, east to Tanjore, south and west over the town, where the streets were all alive with a Mohammedan procession and the beating of drums. Outside the town to the south-west lay the military cantonments, where about five thousand troops are kept; and to the west are the chapels, monasteries and nunneries of the Roman Catholics. Almost all the Tamil servants are said to be Romanists. The Lutherans too have missions here, called the Leipzig Mission, and the new Lutheran church is a conspicuous object. They recognise the laws of caste among their converts. Immediately at the foot of the rock is the chapel in which the well-known missionary, C. F. Schwartz, preached. The old pulpit from which he so often proclaimed the message of Christ to the natives is still there. His influence with the native population was irresistible. In their transactions with the English they would treat only through him. He was born in Germany, on the 26th of October, 1726, and died at Tanjore, on the 14th of February, 1789, "revered," as the tablet in his church there says, "by Christian, Mohammedan, and Hindu alike." He left three thousand converts to Christianity behind him, in Tanjore alone. The remains of another famous Indian missionary, Bishop Heber, lie here in St. John's Church. He died suddenly at Trichinopoly, in 1826, when taking a cold bath, in the forty-third year of his age.

A three miles' drive northwards from Trichinopoly brings you to the famous Dravidian temples of SERINGHAM, the largest in all India. Seringham is a river-island formed by the Kâveri, which, rising far away in the Nilgiri Hills, about five miles above Trichinopoly divides into two branches. The Great Pagoda in the island thus formed is seven miles in circumference, and includes many bazaars and streets of Brahmans' houses, so that it is more like a walled town than a temple. The sight of the fourteen magnificent gate towers or gopuras from the outside is very impressive. Each has huge monoliths of granite on either side, the portico about forty feet high; and above the majestic gateways are pyramids of elaborate stone carving towering up to the height of two hundred feet. You drive through a succession of these gopuras, and alighting, you enter on foot a great choultry or pillared hall whose flat stone roof, fifteen feet high, is supported by one thousand columns, each a single block of granite, and all carved into grotesque figures of men and horses, men mounted upon rearing horses, and spearing tigers, and the like. Beyond is the central shrine, dark and dismal, but surmounted by a golden dome. Near to this four sacred elephants are stabled, and a staircase leads up to the flat stone roof which covers all these acres. The highest gopura was ascended by the Prince of Wales during his tour through India in 1875, and he left a gift of five hundred rupees to the temple. The contrast between the vastness, majesty and grandeur of the temple precincts, embodying the skill and toil of thousands of labourers and

SERINGHAM.

lapidaries for years, and the hideous, dirty, greasy, little idol before the dimly burning lamp in the centre, is most strange and striking. The most laborious and elaborate architecture in the world has been raised in honour of the most hideous idols, and for the most degraded idolatry.

A mile from the walls of this wide-spreading temple is another, smaller but older, namely, the Jambukeswar Pagoda, which is in decay, but is a very compact specimen of Dravidian architecture. As the large temple of Seringham

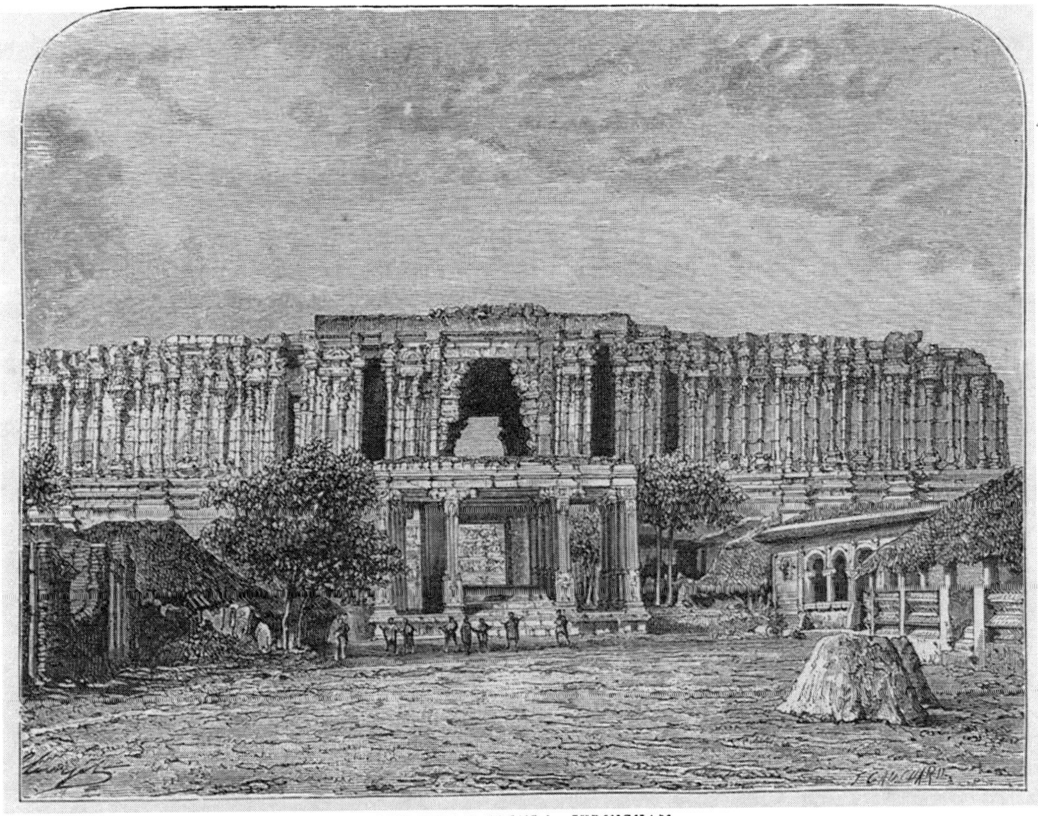

THE RAJAH-GOPURA, SERINGHAM.

is dedicated to Vishnu, this is raised to Siva, and its name denotes him as "Lord of the rose-apple," or "Lord of India."

Looking westward from Trichinopoly, one sees the noble range of the Nilgiri hills, a group of granite mountains shaped like a triangle, and about forty miles in length. Owing to their great elevation (seven thousand feet), they have a delightful climate and are much resorted to. The principal stations are, Coonoor, Wellington and Utakamund. A branch line of railway runs from Coimbatore, near the gap in the mountains of the same name, northwards to Mettapollium ; and thus this healthy and delightful resort is brought within a sixteen hours' journey of Madras itself. Utakamund is the summer seat of the Madras Government. The hills, covered with dark soil and grass, possess a vegetation of the temperate zone, with a mean temperature of 58°. Here live the tribe of Tudas, numbering about two thousand, a handsome race, theists in religion, but with no idols. Three miles from Coimbatore is the

TUDAS IN THE NILGIRIS.

Pagoda of Perur, not of very ancient date, but containing interesting details of architecture, and elaborate compound pillars ; but the subjects of the carving show that degradation which is justly described as "the fatal characteristic of art in India." The excursion to the Anamalai (elephant) hills is healthy and exhilarating. There are now extensive coffee plantations on the slopes of the Nilgiri hills. In the Nilgiris a small but singular tribe of people is

TANJORE.

met with, called TUDAS. They are a handsome race, tall and athletic, with Roman noses, beautiful teeth, and large full expressive eyes. They never wear any head covering, but let the hair grow six or seven inches, so that it forms a thick bushy mass of curls all round. They are honest, brave, inoffensive, and live as herdmen, but are somewhat indolent. Polyandry prevails among them, the brothers of a family having often only one wife among them. Their language is peculiar, but Dravidian. As has been already said, they have no idols; but they have a temple dedicated to *truth*. They regard the Brahmans with contempt. They are considered to be the aborigines of these hills. They only number a few hundred, and are gradually decreasing. The Badaga tribe is more numerous and more accessible to Christian influences.

TEMPLE OF SOUBRAMANYA, TANJORE.

TANJORE is two hours' journey by railway from Trichinopoly; and crowds of natives, with the varying symbols of their caste painted on their foreheads, filled the stations and thronged the carriages. There are first, the Brahmans, or priests, sprung from the mouth of Brahma, distinguished by the sacred cord around their bodies; secondly, the Kshuttries, or warriors, sprung from his arms; third, the Vaisyas, from his thighs, the merchants, men of commerce, industry and agriculture; and fourth, the Sudras, the cultivators of the soil, labourers and servants, sprung from the feet of Brahma. Below these are those of no caste, the Pariahs or outcasts. One sees men of all these several castes crowded together, jostling one another on the railway platform and crowding into the same carriage; for though there are four classes of carriages on Indian railways, many of the highest castes are the poorest, and have to travel fourth class, and you will see the Brahman sitting side by side with the Pariah. The railway is the great antagonist to caste in India.

Tanjore is a large city of a hundred thousand inhabitants. In former times it was the seat of Brahminical learning, and it contains several pagodas in large green areas or gardens, and two large walled forts. As you approach the city, the Great Pagoda with its lofty gopura is a conspicuous object, impressive and graceful. Its base measures eighty feet square, and

PALACE OF THE RAJAHS AT TANJORE.

the pyramid rises fourteen stories to the height of two hundred feet. The top-stone or dome is a huge monolith, beautifully carved and said to weigh eighty tons. The courts are not covered over as at Madura, but are open to light and air, and within the precincts is a large open square six hundred feet by two hundred. Here is the colossal bull Nundi, fifteen feet long and twelve feet high, in a couching posture, of stone saturated with oil. It rests upon a platform which you ascend by twelve steps, and has over it a large canopy supported by granite pillars. This bull, sacred to Siva, faces the magnificent temple, an oblong building of red sandstone, with the huge gopura rising nobly over the shrine. Farther on to the left, but within the enclosure, is another but much smaller shrine, of beautifully carved stone, and cloisters surround the court covered with coarse pictures of heroes. To the right, within the court, is the Temple of Soubramanya, "as exquisite a piece of decorative architecture," says Mr. Fergusson, "as is to be found in the south of India." The steps up to its entrance are supported by small carved elephants with men in singular attitudes, sitting on or falling from their

COURT IN PALACE OF THE RAJAH, TANJORE.

trunks. The palace of the Princess of Tanjore contains an open court, with singular figures in stone, and a statue in white marble of the late Rajah. In the Protestant mission church built by Schwartz, his remains lie, and a slab behind the pulpit with an inscription marks the spot. The country about Tanjore looked peculiarly rich and fertile. The great river Kâveri here opens out into a delta, and irrigation works of considerable extent distribute its fertilising waters.

The Danes were the first among Protestant nations to send the Gospel to India, for in the year 1705 Ziegenbalg came to Tranquebar on the east coast, and made his way to Tanjore, dressed in native costume. The Rajah at first objected, but afterwards sanctioned the mission. Ziegenbalg, having translated the New Testament into Tamil, died in 1719, and his work was resumed by Schultze, and several congregations of Christians grew up in the kingdom of Tanjore. Then followed the war between France and England which ended in the conquests of the latter under Clive, and the chaplaincy of the garrison of Trichinopoly by the equally eminent soldier, although of the Prince of Peace, the well-known Schwartz, whom the Rajah requested to remove from Trichinopoly and to reside at Tanjore. Here he was employed upon several occasions to treat with the native princes. "Let them send the Christian," said they; "he will not deceive us." On two occasions, when

BHISTI, OR WATER-CARRIER.

the Fort of Tanjore was threatened with famine, and the Rajah was powerless to obtain supplies, Schwartz, at his earnest request, undertook to relieve it, and succeeded in saving its inmates from starvation. A few hours before his death the Rajah requested Schwartz to act as guardian to his infant son. Schwartz in fact was revered as a father by the people as well as by the Rajah of Tanjore. The Tanjore mission was his chief work, and he continued its guiding spirit to the end. At his death in 1798, after forty-eight years spent in the country, a long and bitter cry of lamentation arose from multitudes, and the Rajah shed a flood of tears over his body, and covered it with a gold cloth. The Christian Knowledge Society sustained the mission after Schwartz's death, and the Leipzig missionaries commended their Christianity to the Hindus by the adoption of caste, a step which has made the prosecution of Christian work very difficult. But the Propagation Society has nine central missions in the provinces of Tanjore and Trichinopoly, and at Combaconum there are many converts, though chiefly from the lower castes.

The new railway between Tanjore and Madras was not yet complete, the bridges over the estuary of one of the rivers (the Peravanur) not being built; and in the middle of the night we were conveyed in bullock waggons inland and across this estuary, thus giving us an idea of what travelling must have been in the country before railways were made. The entire journey is about two hundred miles, and it is now accomplished in eighteen hours, four of which were occupied in the bullock waggon over half-a-dozen miles.

The line runs along the tract of country long known as the Coromandel Coast, which stretches for about four hundred miles north from Adam's Bridge. Throughout its whole extent this coast does not afford any secure port or harbour. A heavy surf rolls in upon the flat sandy shore. The soil near the coast is a mixture of sea-sand and loam, often in dry weather covered with salt. Farther inland low hills commence, and the soil when irrigated is fertile, but the upper part of the hills is sterile.

This coast, though destitute of harbours, has been the favourite country for European settlements. Here is PONDICHERRY, still belonging to the French, divided into two portions, the white town orderly, neat, with beautiful boulevards, the black, or native town, with a large pagoda. Its lower or square part is quite plain, but from its cornice upwards there are large and fantastic figures, those in the centre somewhat resembling Buddha, and indicating the influence of his system even in South India. No doubt the gopura has undergone alteration and repair, for in portions figures are introduced representing European soldiers. In fact, nothing can be too fantastic for these carvings; figures the most grotesque and caricatures are introduced. The summit seems to represent the *trisula* ornament, symbolical of the Buddhist trinity.

Pondicherry is a town of fifty thousand inhabitants, including about a thousand Europeans. The *Missions étrangères de France* have a settlement here. They are successful among the natives; but they conform in great part to their idolatrous customs and caste prejudices. The priests have assumed the character of Brahmans of a superior caste from the Western world. In fact, at one time they were wont to wear the *cavy*, or orange robe peculiar to the most venerated Brahmans, and carried on their foreheads the sacred spot of sandal-wood powder. "If," says the Abbé Dubois, "any mode of Christian worship is calculated to gain ground in India, it is no doubt the Catholic form, which Protestants consider idolatry. Its external pomp and show are well suited to the genius of the natives. It has a *pooja*, or sacrifice, viz. the mass; processions, images, and statues; *tirtan*, or holy water; feasts, fasts, and prayers for the dead; invocation of saints, and other practices which bear more or less resemblance to that of the Hindus."

Here, too, is Cuddalore, now a handsome town of forty thousand inhabitants, formerly belonging to the French, but yielded by treaty in 1795. Here again is Tranquebar, once a Danish settlement. The entire district abounds in specimens of Dravidian architecture. Far south by Paumban Passage is the great Pagoda of Ramessveram, exhibiting all the beauties of the Dravidian style, with four stone gopuras and corridors with columns elaborately carved.

PAGODA AT PONDICHERRY.

On the railway, twenty-four miles north-east from Tanjore, we pass Combaconum, a town of forty-five thousand inhabitants, one of the old capitals of the native Chola kingdom, once called the Oxford of Southern India, on account of its learning, with its richly ornamented gopura, twelve

GOPURA AT COMBACONUM

stories and one hundred and fifty feet high. The Chola kingdom was one of that tri-archy of kingdoms which existed in South India in the time of Asoka, and down to the Mohammedan conquest, the other two being the Chêra and the Pândya. The large pagoda here is dedicated to Vishnu, another indication of Buddhist influence, for Siva is the favourite deity of the south, and Vishnuism is (as Mr. Fergusson observes) a bad and corrupt form of Buddhism. The great gopura can be ascended, but the stone steps are old and broken, and there is no hand-rail; the floors are of

PAGODA OF CHILLAMBARAM: INTERIOR COURT.

stone, and shake alarmingly to the tread. Near the temple is a large sacred tank into which it is said that the Ganges flows every year. So vast is the concourse of people who descend into the water to bathe at one time, that the surface rises some inches, and this confirms their belief in the miracle. The idol cars are drawn through the streets, as at Puri, and every year persons are accidentally crushed beneath their wheels. The tank is surrounded by a number of small pagodas, each containing a *lingam*. The Beauchamp College at Combaconum is one of the best educational institutions in South

India, and there is a very good school for girls, with upwards of a hundred scholars. Farther north is Chillambaram, where is a very large tank, and at the four cardinal points, four vast gopuras, together with the usual hall of a thousand pillars. On the west of the tank is the Temple of Parvati, sixty-eight feet high, and on the south the Temple of Siva, containing the sacred image of the dancing Siva; the roof is covered with plates of copper gilt. This temple is reputed to be one of the most ancient of the Dravidian pagodas. It is highly venerated by the people, who believe it to be the work of a king in the sixth century whose name signifies "golden-coloured emperor." The tradition is that he was a leper, but miraculously recovered by bathing in the sacred waters of the tank at Chillambaram, and in gratitude he rebuilt the temple. The outer wall is six hundred yards by five hundred, and in the centre lies the celebrated tank around which the buildings cluster. The four points of the compass are marked by four large gopuras. In the sixteenth century the kings of the tri-archy made many donations to the fane. The oldest thing now existing is, in Mr. Fergusson's judgment, a little shrine in the inmost enclosure with a little porch of two pillars, more graceful and more elegantly executed than any other of their class. A chain cut out of solid stone connects two similar and corresponding pillars, upon which dancing figures are engraved in honour of Venna, the god of dancing, of Kashmir, with whom a legend has connected the building. A double gallery with plain and chaste columns runs along the interior enclosure wall. But the most elegant workmanship is found in the porch of the Temple of Parvati, the central aisle of which is seven yards wide. Here the architect has put forth all his power. The temple is an aggregate of buildings of different styles of architecture, and portions could not have been raised till after the Mohammedans had settled in the south and taught the Hindus their methods. It is of granite, and now covers thirty-nine acres of ground.

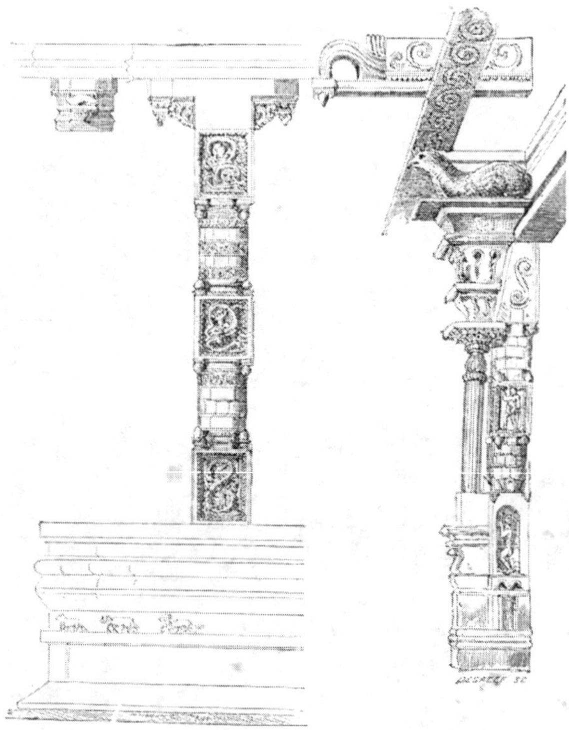

SPECIMENS OF SCULPTURE ON PILLARS, IN THE GRAND GALLERY, CHILLAMBARAM.

At CONJEVERAM, one of the seven holy cities of India, and the Benares of the south, once a city of the Hindu kingdom of Chola, there are two groups of temples, with commanding gopuras nearly two hundred feet high. A symbol like a horse-shoe on the wall of the inner enclosure is said to be the first letter of the word Vishnu, and there has been hard fighting for nearly a century about the form of this symbol; indeed, the Tamils are still at law about it. The one party contend that the mark or symbol—made with a kind of white paint on the forehead—should be made with a plain line, while the other party make it with a little boss at the bottom extending halfway down the nose! These are the two sects of the Vishnuvites. The usual mark worn by the Vishnu worshippers is two *perpendicular* strokes meeting below in a curve; that of the Siva worshippers is quite different, consisting of three *horizontal* lines, usually white. The town of Conjeveram is full of fine trees and low houses. Fantastic figures in wood in the thousand-pillared hall are carried in procession on festival occasions. A large number of *nautch* girls are kept in this temple. The gopuras are full of chambers, but all unoccupied. This is strange, for their great height must conduce to airiness and coolness. But when asked, the Brahmans said they dared not sleep there, for fear of being attacked by evil spirits, ghosts of Brahmans turned into devils; and they used both the Sanscrit and English word explaining the forms as high-caste devils.

CHAIN CUT OUT OF A SINGLE STONE; PILLARS 27 FT. APART, CHILLAMBARAM.

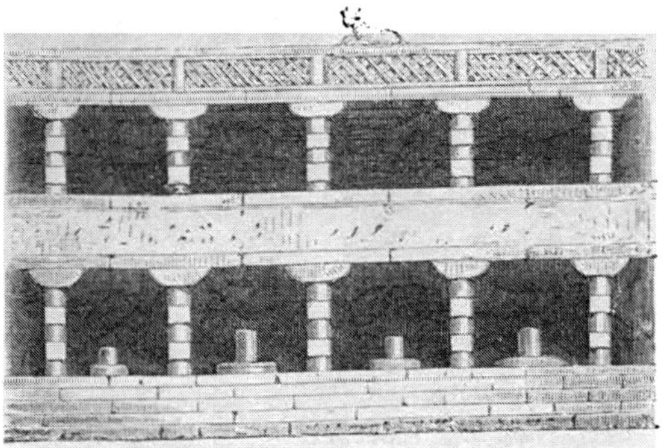

DOUBLE GALLERY, CHILLAMBARAM.

About three hours before reaching Madras (forty miles south), on the coast, are the ruins of an extensive town cut in rock, and called Mahavalipur, or the Seven Pagodas. Here are many curious excavations and carvings in the rock,—groups of monkeys, the boar's temple representing Vishnu as a boar,—the tiger's cave, a cave surrounded with tiger's heads carved in the rock. Another singularly sculptured rock, forty feet high and twice as long, presents a hundred strange figures of men, women, monkeys and elephants. The shore temple is washed by the waves, and the legend tells of many similar buildings partially submerged.

Southey, in his *Curse of Kehama*, refers to this legend of a submerged city thus:

"The sepulchres
Of ancient kings which Bali in his power
Made in primeval times, and built above them
A city like the city of the gods,
Being a god himself. For many an age

ENTRANCE TO THE PAGODA, CONJEVERAM.

Hath ocean warred against his palaces,
Till overwhelmed beneath the waves—
Not overthrown—so well the awful chief
Had laid their deep foundations.

* * * *

Their golden summits in the noonday light
Shone o'er the dark green deep that rolled between,
Her domes and pinnacles and spires were seen
Peering above the sea, a mournful sight.
And on the sandy shore, beside the verge
Of ocean, here and there a rock-cut fane
Resisted in its strength the surf and surge
That on their deep foundations beat in vain."

Mahavalipur is, according to Mr. Fergusson, a petrified Buddhist village, applied to the purposes of another religion, but representing Buddhist forms in the seventh century, when Buddhism was dying out. Doubtless it had some connection with Ceylon. The people who carved these curious monuments seem, says Mr. F., suddenly to have settled on a spot where no temples existed before, and to have set to work at once to fashion the detached granite boulders they found on the shore into nine raths or miniature

MAHAVALIPUR: THE CHAITIYA.

temples. They pierced the side of the hill with fourteen caves, carved two long bas-reliefs, and then abandoned them unfinished. The raths are close together on the sandy beach south of the hill of caves. The largest, called Bhima's Ratha, is sixteen yards long, eight wide, and nine high. The roofs are ornamented with ranges of little recesses or simulated cells, which characterise the Dravidian temples, and are surmounted by a dome, an equally universal feature. The next rath is pyramidal and four stories high. These singular ruins, while they are memorials of Buddhism in its decay, throw light

GREAT RATH AT MAHAVALIPUR.

upon the history of the Dravidian buildings, which probably were originally of wood, and from about the seventh century began to be constructed in stone.

DETAILS OF ENTRANCES TO SUBTERRANEAN TEMPLES, MAHAVALIPUR.

Regarding the Hinduism of Southern India as embodied in these temples, Dr. Monier Williams says: "Religion is even more closely interwoven with every affair of daily life, and is even more showily demonstrative in the south of India than in the north. A distinction must be pointed out between Brahmanism and Hinduism. Brahmanism is the purely pantheistic and not necessarily idolatrous creed evolved by the Brahmans out of the religion of the Veda. Hinduism is that complicated system of polytheistic doctrines, idolatrous superstitions, and caste usages which has been developed out of Brahmanism after its contact with Buddhism and its admixture with the non-Aryan creeds of the Dravidians and aborigines of Southern India. Brahmanism and Hinduism, though infinitely remote from each other, are integral parts of the same system. One is the germ or root, the other is the rank and diseased outgrowth. . . . Vaishnavism and Saivism (or the worship of Vishnu and Siva) constitute the very heart and soul of Southern Hinduism. As to Brahma, the third member of the Hindoo Triad, and original creator of the world, he is not worshipped at all, except in the person of his alleged offspring, the Brahmans. Moreover, Vaishnavism and Saivism are nowhere so pronounced and imposing as in Southern India. The temples of Conjeveram, Tanjore, Trichinopoly, Madura, Tinnevelly, and Ramessveram are as superior in magnitude to those of Benares as Westminster Abbey and St. Paul's are to the other churches of London. Furthermore, it must not be forgotten that although a belief in devils, and homage to *bhutas*, or spirits of all kinds, are common all over India, yet what is called 'devil worship' is far more systematically practised in the South of India and in Ceylon than in the North. The god Siva is constantly connected with demoniacal agencies, either as superintending and controlling them, or as himself possessing (especially in the person of his wife Kali) all the fierceness and malignity usually attributed to demons. . . . All honour to those noble-hearted missionaries who are seeking by the establishment of female schools to supply India with its most pressing need—good wives and mothers—and are training girls to act as high-class schoolmistresses, and sending them forth to form new centres of female education in various parts of Southern India."

ENTRANCES TO SUBTERRANEAN TEMPLES, MAHAVALIPUR.

No city, perhaps, in the world has a site so utterly unpropitious and disadvantageous as MADRAS. On a coast exposed without shelter to the north-east monsoon, with a barrier of sand lashed continually by a surf passable in fine weather only by native boats of singular construction manned by native boatmen, and in foul weather insurmountable even by these, with no navigable river flowing into the sea, it spreads along the border of a wilderness of barren sand in the torrid zone, exposed to the unsheltered glare of a scorching sun. The first British settlement was at Armagan, sixty miles north, a situation with some natural advantages, where a factory was built; but in 1639 the East India Company's agent abandoned it for the miserable spot, granted in irony by a native prince, upon which he built Fort St. George. Nothing more strikingly illustrates the power of British pluck and enterprise than the present aspect of Madras. Along that inhospitable coast for a distance of nine miles, and covering that sandy waste, there now stretches a thriving city, with an area of twenty-seven square miles, and a population of four hundred thousand. Along that unprotected roadstead the ships of all nations ride at anchor to take in or discharge cargo; and from the city the iron horse wends its way north-westerly across the continent, eight hundred miles in forty hours, to Bombay, and sends its tracks southwards almost to Cape Comorin. The meridian of Madras now gives its time to the entire railway system of India.

TIGER CAVE, MAHAVALIPUR.

Spreading over this wide area, Madras is an aggregation of no less than twenty-three towns and villages, with public buildings, European residences, warehouses and even shops in park-like enclosures, filling up the intervening spaces. Beginning with the north, there is Royapuram, with the Tinnevelly settlement; then the Black Town, defended from the encroachments of the sea by a strong stone bulwark, and with seven wells of water, filtered through the sand, pure and wholesome. The population of these two is one hundred and fifty thousand. Next comes Fort St. George, the first nucleus of the city, strongly fortified, containing the arsenal, council house, and the Fort church, with its monument to the missionary Schwartz; and beyond, the island and the Governor's house and gardens. Then southwards, Triplicane, the Mohammedan quarter, with eighty thousand souls; and beyond this St. Thomé, the traditional site of the martyrdom of the Apostle Thomas. Inland, beyond the Fort and the Black Town, are Chintadrepettah and Vepery, in which stands the church where the Lutheran missionary Sartorius preached for many years, and where the London Mission has its compound. The view from the lighthouse, one hundred and eleven feet high, is extensive; one sees the entire city, and the shore for miles. The houses for the most part are yellow, covered with the stucco called chunam, which when dried and polished has the appearance of the finest

ENTRANCE TO ROCK TEMPLE, MAHAVALIPUR.

marble. The grounds round the European houses are well planted, and the country now presents a green and cheerful aspect. Mount Road, running south and inland, leads to many bungalows and hotels. The drive along the beach to the Capper House is the pleasantest in Madras. Here one meets the sea-breeze, appropriately called by the residents "the doctor." Here we pass the most imposing of the public buildings of the city, in particular the University. It was strange to see on the Sunday the punkas swinging during service in the churches. Like huge weavers' beams with heavy curtains, they are kept in motion by means of cords pulled from the outside, two natives, who keep each other

SELLERS OF MILK, MADRAS.

awake, being employed for every one. However strict a Sabbatarian, the minister as well as the people must have the punka kept going over his head throughout the service.

In Madras we visited two large hospitals; the one in the Foreign Town supported by Europeans and conducted upon the English system, the other in the Native Town and under native superintendence. The general hospital in the Foreign Town is a very large and well-ventilated building. It has spacious corridors, wide and shady verandas, and noble wards. The doors were open on every hand, mainly towards the verandas; and a refreshing breeze passing gently through, relieved the heat, which in this climate is so oppressive to the patient. In every ward freshness and cheerfulness seemed to bespeak a cure. Hopefulness was upon the countenances even of the most afflicted, and pleasant pictures and beautiful flowers gladdened the eye. The matron is a lady clever and kind. Her apartments are at the top of the building, on which a garden is laid out, and which commands an extensive view. The other hospital, that in the Black Town, was, I regret to say, a contrast to all this. It is called the Choultry Poor-house and Hospital. Here mute misery was written on every face. The patients had no bedclothes. The paupers lie on a mat on the floor. The portion set apart for lepers presented a most painful spectacle. Those who were in the early stages of the disease were all oiled, and were sitting on their haunches, rubbing and scratching themselves uneasily. Two young men, brothers, presented two different types of the disease. The one was not in the least disfigured; the other was frightfully so, the face being covered with blotches. But whatever the form it assumes, the disease is incurable. In its later stages ulcers appear, and eat off fingers and toes, features and limbs. Several poor wretches in great suffering were plastering their own sores, the materials for doing so being handed to them at the point of a long wand. It was a revolting sight. Most of the sufferers were natives, but a few knew English. To these I spoke a few words about the Lord Jesus and the lepers. It was all one could then do. Sickened and saddened, we next went through bare and comfortless wards for aged and infirm men and women, who here drag out the residue of their days of sorrow. There is also a foundling ward. The foundlings seemed to be in great wretchedness. In this hospital there were 250 patients, and the average was at that time ten deaths a week.

During the awful famine of 1878, there were nine thousand inmates, kept in a sort of camp, and an average of thirty deaths a day. The dead were burnt in heaps by contract daily. In this lazar house there were, when we visited it, 250 patients in hospital, 275 in the almshouses, 42 in the Rajah's Choultry, and 250 lepers; making a total of 817 souls. The horrors of that famine year are untold and untellable. As the waggons of grain passed from the shore to the railway, they had to be guarded with a strong military force; but the starving would risk blows of sabres and horses' hoofs to pierce the sacks, so that the grain might trickle out; and afterwards hundreds might be seen eagerly picking up the grains that had fallen upon the road. In punishment for this offence all who could be captured were driven into pens set up upon the shore, and confined there without food or water, and under the blaze of the sun, for four and twenty hours. Thus many perished. And this was not in remote districts, but at the head-quarters of British power, pomp and fashion in South India—in Madras itself! Inland they died of famine by hundreds. "I do not know," said an eyewitness, a government dispenser of relief, "I do not know what we should have done without the dogs and vultures."

PORTION OF GOPURA AT TIRUPETTY.

No account of Madras would be complete without a reference to the Free Church College, which stands first among the educational establishments of Southern India. It was begun in 1837 by the well-known missionary Dr. Anderson,—whose name is in the south what the name of Dr. Duff is in the north,—and within a year there were two hundred and seventy scholars. But then it was suddenly broken up by the agency of "that hydra-headed monster," Caste. Two Pariah boys were admitted, and the rest left. Dr. Anderson was entreated to dismiss the Pariah boys, but he was firm; and he gained the victory. By-and-by the youths returned; and Pariah and Brahman might be seen sitting side by side on the same bench, learning the same lessons. This was a blow given to caste that has been felt throughout Southern India, and felt to the present day. The numbers soon rose to five hundred; and ever since the college has maintained its position as the most efficient in Madras. It is a striking fact that the three Presidency cities in India—Madras, Calcutta, and Bombay—possess colleges organised by Scotchmen, which have accomplished greater results in producing an enlightened and well-trained body of natives in India than any other society, nay more, than the Government itself.

At Tirupetty, about fifty miles from Madras, there is an old temple much frequented by pilgrims, and very interesting to the student of Indian architecture. Pursuing the path up the hill, we go through three gopuras curiously carved. The hill is two thousand five hundred feet high, and has seven peaks or summits, on the last of which is the pagoda. Along the top are ruined houses, forming a quadrangle, with stone wall enclosure. A tower rises above these, and around is a broad belt of mango, tamarind, and sandal trees. It is said to be one of the oldest Dravidian temples.

West of Madras about sixty miles is Arcot, the famous town which Clive pounced upon in 1751, that he might relieve Trichinopoly. The garrison, seeing Clive's troops marching on steadily in the teeth of a thunder-storm, thought they were fire-proof, and abandoned the place. Entering it, Clive held the place during a fifty days' siege, and repelled the assaults of the Mohammedan troops. Arcot is now a large and prosperous town. Beyond lies MYSORE, one of the most flourishing of the native tributary states in India, occupying a table-land lofty, well-wooded and cool, where is the famous Seringapatam, now almost in ruins, and Bangalore, one of the healthiest cities in India, with a large British settlement. Scattered over the table-land are many huge isolated rocks called *drûgs*, four thousand feet above the sea, and formerly used as fortresses. Coorg is a mountainous district, thickly-wooded, with extensive coffee and tea plantations. Worthiest of record is the name of a native, Samuel Flavel, a man of great originality, intellectual power and untiring zeal, who for twenty years (1826–1847), was instrumental in spreading Christianity with its civilising influences in Mysore.

MADRAS SURF.

The coast voyage from Madras to Calcutta occupies eight days, and gives an opportunity of seeing the main ports, the steamer calling daily at some place on the way, and stopping four or six hours. Of the entire voyage the most difficult and disagreeable part often is the passage over the surf from the shore to the ship. The morning was calm; yet the huge billows were rolling in in all their majesty and strength. There lay our Masulah boat waiting to receive us. These boats are twenty-five feet long, eight feet broad, and six feet deep. They are flat-bottomed and pointed and curved up high at either end. They are exceedingly light, and draw only three inches of water. There is not a nail in them nor a rib of timber; they are sewn together with cocoa-nut fibre, and padded inside with straw, outside with tow. They yield to the force of the wave and to the bump of the shore. As they lie on the sand, they seem to you immovable; but the native boatmen, twelve in number, soon push their obedient and easily managed craft to the advancing lip of the wave; it is carried out as this retreats, and they dexterously jump in, lay hold of their paddles, and pull with their might. The helmsman steers with a long and powerful oar, and thus keeps the bow to the waves. And now you see approaching the next yawning wave high above you, and threatening to engulf you; but meeting it, the sloping bow mounts up perpendicularly, shipping perhaps a quantity of spray, but springing first to the top and then over the crest of the huge billow, and down again into the shallow water left as the wave rolls on. In calm weather only three of these huge billows are dangerous, and these surmounted, you are safe. But the boatmen have been trained to the work from boyhood, and handle their craft with marvellous skill. Though a daily feat, the novelty seems never to wear off. They are all excitement, and cheer over each leap and plunge. Besides the Masulah boats, another kind of craft is used by the natives, called a catamaran, which is simply a raft constructed of three pieces of timber ten or twelve feet long, tied together, the middle one being longer than the others and curved upwards at the ends. It is driven through the surf by a man with a paddle, who is often washed off, but is so well practised that he leaps on again in an instant. With these amphibious creatures the catamaran keeps on its way where a boat would inevitably be lost. It took us half an hour in the Masulah boat to reach our ship, the boatmen keeping time to a monotonous song.

The first port off which we anchored on our coasting voyage northwards was Masulipatam. Masulipatam is a very old and important city of forty thousand inhabitants, situated in the Telugu District, and between the deltas of the two mighty rivers, the Krishna and the Godavery. Telugu is the most melodious and soft of the Dravidian languages, and is spoken throughout the portion of the Madras Presidency extending northward to Orissa. It is also spoken far inland in the Nizam's dominions. The great rivers, the Krishna (or Kistna) and the Godavery form the characteristic physical features of the country. Both rise in the Western Ghauts, seventy miles north-west of Bombay, the Godavery near Nassick, and they sweep across the vast table-land from west to east, flowing right across the Indian peninsula, winding their way by deep defiles through the Eastern Ghauts, and spreading over the country in immense deltas as they empty themselves into the sea. Formerly these rivers were a peril to the country, overflowing their banks and sweeping whole villages away. But the irrigation works of modern enterprise "have turned the furious streams into ministering angels." Colossal *anicuts*, or dams, have with immense labour been thrown across them, and the water is carried by canals over the whole country, which has thus become one of the richest grain-producing districts in India. Masulipatam possesses a cotton manufacture, distinguished for the bright and beautiful colours of its cloth. In the centre of the city, where the streets meet, are thirty-three huge limestone slabs covered with alto- and bas-reliefs brought from the ruins of a neighbouring pagoda. Masulipatam is the centre of the operations of the Church Missionary Society in this part of India; the noble High School for the thorough education of young Hindus is distinguished in influence and success, and its pupils are to be found in almost every department, as sub-magistrates, schoolmasters and even deputy collectors. Inland, at Guntur, the American Lutherans have a flourishing mission. In this district are the Buddhist topes of Amravati, fragments of which are in the British Museum. The rails are the most richly ornamented in India, and furnish a series of pictures of Buddhism, "unsurpassed" says Fergusson, "by anything now known to exist in India."

Another night's voyage brought us northwards to Cocanada, north of the river in the Godavery District, where we spent our second day. Landing in the morning, we made our way to the compound of the Canadian Baptist Mission, delightfully shaded with banyan and pipul trees, and there we heard much of the marvellous conversions at Nellore and Ongole, where eight thousand natives had in one month embraced Christianity, owing to Christian kindness during the famine. Here we travelled inland about five miles in coffin-like palanquins, with twelve bearers to each, who went dolefully along on the high banks of a canal keeping time with their voices in the heat of the day, to a lonely pagoda whose towering gopura is a

PALMYRAS IN THE GODAVERY.

revolting sight. It is, in fact, a mass of obscenity cut in stone, such as one could hardly imagine depravity itself capable of inventing. Yet this is connected with, nay, is part and parcel of the religion of Brahma; that religion upon the excellency of which some Sanscrit professors expatiate! One sight of this temple at Cocanada would suffice to disabuse them of their fine pictures of Hinduism and of the elevating power of the Vedas. A few pet quotations are always at hand when one would praise Brahmanism. They are in the oldest Vedas, grains of wheat in the bushel of chaff. If we would learn what the Hindu religion really is, and what are its practical fruits, we must visit the temples of India.

Next morning we reached Vizagapatam, or Vizag, as it is briefly called. The headland (one thousand seven hundred feet), as approached from the

DURBAR OF A NATIVE PRINCE IN THE SOUTH OF THE DECCAN.

south, is called the Dolphin's Nose; there is a huge cave on the sea-line, and the cliffs are imposing. On the hill above the creek three striking buildings meet the eye — a heathen temple, a Mohammedan mosque, and a Roman Catholic church. As we landed, we saw crowds of poor women working as porters, and carrying huge boxes of cargo. Vizagapatam is in the province called the Northern Circars, extending about five hundred miles along the Bay of Bengal and among the earliest possessions of the East India Company. The natives are a fine class of men, both in physique and

BRAHMAN PREPARED FOR PRAYERS.

in character, and live under the simple form of village government. The country about Vizagapatam is hilly and picturesque, and there is a Hindu temple of great fame and antiquity at Semachillum. The London Mission here was founded in 1805, at a time when the Company discountenanced missions. But it has held its ground, and its missionaries have translated the Scriptures into Telugu. I met the venerable John Hay, the chief translator, and master of the language, who has been here for forty years. The Telugu language is, Mr. Hay says, in its primitive forms, much simpler than in its more modern development. On account of its soft accent and musical tones, it has been called by Europeans the Italian of the East.

Our next day was spent in discharging cargo at Gopalpur, a small uninteresting village upon a sandy beach, up which a heavy surf rolls. The natives come out in their Masulah boats, like tolerably water-tight wooden baskets stitched together with rope, and wonderfully light and springy. Eight miles from Gopalpur is Berhampur, chief town of the district of Ganjam, and beyond is the Mahendra range, noted for its woods, its cairn-like temples, built up of huge rough blocks, and four thousand nine hundred feet above the sea. The outside of the chief building is ornamented with figures, and the roof is covered with vegetation. At Berhampur there is a flourishing Baptist Mission. This district forms the extreme north of the Madras Presidency.

Inland, and behind the strip of the Madras Presidency, running up thus far north along the coast, are two large tracts of territory, the CENTRAL PROVINCES, now belonging to Britain, and HAIDARABAD, belonging to the Nizam of the Deccan. The district called the Central Provinces is not thickly peopled, the country being hilly and forest land. The chief town, Nagpur, contains about eighty thousand inhabitants. There are extensive coal-fields, and cotton is much cultivated. The Deccan is a name applied to the entire central plateau of the Indian Peninsula, of which Haidarabad forms the northern portion. The Vindhya Mountains, running east and west, form a great wall, separating the Deccan and the Ganges valley. They extend from Mount Parasnath in the east to Mount Abu in the west. Near the city of Haidarabad is the British settlement called Secunderabad, eighteen hundred feet above the sea, where are the largest barracks in India. The Godavery river flows through this district eastward, and it is crossed by the railway connecting Madras with Bombay. Not far from Haidarabad is Golconda; and near the fort, on the top of a conical hill, the tombs of the kings are well worth a visit. Their vastness and solidity are most impressive. The diamonds of Golconda were merely cut and polished here, being found at Partial. Chanda stands amid charming scenery. The Free Church of Scotland has flourishing missions at Nagpur and at the settlement called Jalna, a British cantonment in the Nizam's dominions.

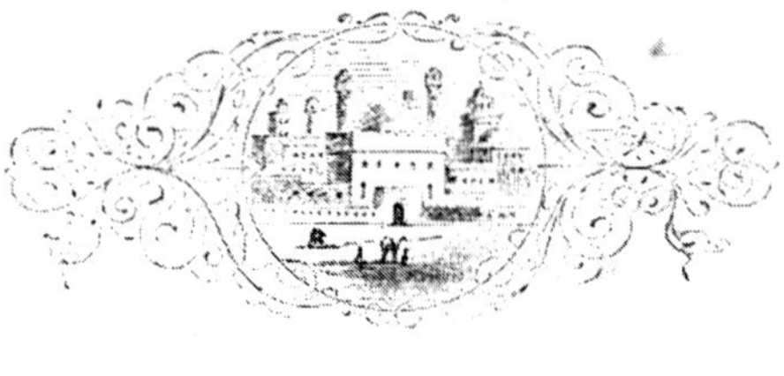

TEMPLE OF JUGGERNAUT.

THE BENGAL PROVINCES.

THE BENGAL PROVINCES.

ORISSA AND JUGGERNAUT—CALCUTTA AND ITS SURROUNDINGS—BARRACKPORE—SERAMPORE—DARJEELING AND THE HIMÂLAYAS—THE GREAT GANGETIC PLAIN.

HIMÂLAYAN WOMAN.

IN the coasting voyage from Madras we have the Madras Presidency still to our port, or left hand, northwards as far as Gopalpur. Here the country of the Northern Circars ends, and the coast of Orissa begins. The maritime part of Orissa forms the British district of Cuttack, called by seamen the Orissa Coast. The shore is flat and dreary, and inland appear several "saddle-hills" terminating in a chain of mountains running south. The extensive Chilka Lake is joined to the sea by a narrow strait.

After leaving Gopalpur, our good steamer keeping near to shore, brought us next morning to Puri in Orissa, and the far-famed Temple of Juggernaut. This part of the coast is considered healthy, and the sea breeze is found very refreshing. The houses of English residents are on the sea-shore, and the native town and temple, surrounded by high wall and luxuriant vegetation, lie a little inland. The temple enclosure measures four hundred and twenty by three hundred and fifteen feet, and the height of the great tower is one hundred and ninety-two feet. "Whitewash and paint," says Mr. Fergusson, "have done their worst to add vulgarity to forms already sufficiently ungraceful, and this, the most famous, is also the most disappointing of Northern Hindu temples." It was erected in A.D. 1174, and is the latest of the Orissa group of temples. It is dedicated to Vishnu, and pilgrims are continually on their way through Bengal to and from this temple. It is calculated that ten thousand pilgrims annually die either of disease or fatigue and want at Puri, or on the return journey. Those who live bring back with them umbrellas made of cane and palm-leaves, bundles of painted rattan canes, and backbones of cuttle-fish, to show that they have been on the sea-shore. These fish-bones are called by the poetic name of "ocean foam." The street leading to the temple is full of sacred buildings, and the inhabitants of the town number thirty thousand. Three wooden images of revolting aspect, six feet high, represent the god Juggernaut, his brother, and his sister; and once a year, in the month of March, these are taken through the town, each idol in its car, that of Juggernaut being thirty-four feet high, with sixteen wheels. On these occasions a hundred and fifty thousand pilgrims are assembled. The English Government has interfered to put an end to the self-immolations beneath its wheels. Mounted police armed with heavy whips accompany the car in its progress, and when a frenzied devotee throws himself in its way the whip is applied, and he immediately jumps up and runs away, forgetting that if he is willing to be killed he should be willing to bear the lash. The tradition of a bone of Krishna being contained in the image is regarded as a Brahmanical form of Buddhist relic-worship, and the three images are supposed to be only the Buddhist trinity, Buddha, Dharma, Sanga. The idol is, in fact, an imitation of the Buddhist emblem. Buddhism formerly existed in Orissa, and the tooth-relic of Buddha was preserved at Puri. Everything at Puri is redolent of Buddhism. Another significant vestige of this system is the absence of all recognition of caste during the festivals. In the neighbourhood of Juggernaut, on the coast, is the so-called Black Pagoda at Kanarak, of which only the beautiful three-storied porch remains, carved with elegance and variety. Orissa, indeed, abounds with temples, all of the same type, and very different from those of Southern India. The towers, or vimanas, have a curved outline; they are not storied, and the buildings have no pillars. The Temple of Juggernaut is the latest, and the oldest is supposed to be the great Temple of Bhuvaneswar.

"The Temple of Bhuvaneswar is," says Fergusson, "perhaps the finest example of a purely Hindu temple in India." It is three hundred feet long by seventy-five broad. It consisted of a vimana, or tower, and a porch. It has a singularly solemn and pleasing aspect. Its height is

BLACK PAGODA AT KANARAK, ORISSA.

one hundred and eighty feet, wholly of stone, and every inch of the surface is covered with elaborate carving. "Infinite labour bestowed on every detail was the mode in which a Hindu thought he could render his temple most worthy of the deity, and, whether he was right or wrong, the effect of the whole is marvellously beautiful."

On Sunday, as we were passing Juggernaut Puri, our ship's company of passengers and officers were quietly gathered on deck to offer our common prayers to the great Father in heaven, to read His Word and to hear His Gospel. Again it was my lot to conduct service at sea, and the heaving of the ship formed a natural accompaniment to the lessons and the sermon. On board was an officer high in rank, and inspector of military schools, who spoke of what he had seen of the brutal treatment of the natives. A passing Hindu, he said, was rudely taken to task by Captain —— for not making a salaam to him. "Why should I?" said the man; "you have conquered our race, and I won't salaam." "Let us see the general," said the captain. The general said, "Make a salaam, sir." The man still firmly but calmly refused, and the general seized him by the neck, threw him to the ground, buried his face in the dust, and ordered the man fifty lashes. Thus by sheer brute force was this Hindu punished for an independence which we should honour in an Englishman. The mild Hindu submits to the English as to a conquering race, and all he can do is to be patient and bide his time. If not subdued by justice and kindness, he will seek his revenge some day.

In the afternoon we anchored at False Point, outside the mud-locked harbour at the mouth of the Mahanadi river. It is a dismal spot, with a house on the beach and a lighthouse in the distance. A few cargo boats and native vessels were swinging at anchor and rolling lazily with the tide. From this place a steam-launch runs, or rather crawls up the river to Cuttack, the capital of Orissa, whither some of our passengers were bound. When Akbar built Attock (or Attack) on the Indus, *Kattack* and *Attack* were spoken of as the two extremes of the Mogul Empire. Seventy miles beyond Cuttack is the famous Barmul Pass, eight miles long, between peaked ridges and hills covered with jungle, through which the Mahanadi flows rapidly. The scenery is said somewhat to resemble the Lower Danube.

And now weighing anchor, and taking our pilot on board, we started up that narrow and dangerous branch of the Ganges called the Hoogly. After stopping at Diamond Harbour, a turn or reach in the river with its signal flagstaff, where particulars are given as to the height of the tide at the bars, we made our way cautiously up past "James and Mary," the most dangerous of the rapids, all hands on board being in readiness to let go the anchor, if we should ground. At Garden Reach our ship was turned round, and was steamed stern foremost up to Government House, CALCUTTA, amidst a crowd of shipping reminding one of Liverpool.

Calcutta, ninety miles from the sea, and on the east bank of the Hoogly, which here flows directly south, is a city not two centuries old. It was founded by Job Charnock, who set up a factory here in 1690, married a

PAGODA NEAR CUTTACK.

Hindu wife, and as to religion led a Hindu life. In 1742 the famous ditch was cut to protect the settlement against the Mahratta cavalry. It ran along the ground now marked by the Circular Road. The settlement, in spite of this, was captured by the Nawab, when, on the 19th of June, 1756, a

GRAND TEMPLE OF BHUVANESWAR.

hundred and forty-six Europeans were imprisoned in the Black Hole, a small chamber eighteen feet square in the Fort, and one hundred and twenty-three were smothered to death. The Black Hole was destroyed in 1818. In January of 1757 Clive won back the settlement; and the place has gradually grown in size and importance until now it is the centre of Government, the seat of the Viceroy, and if we include Howrah, on the opposite bank of the river, now connected with the city by a bridge, it numbers nine hundred thousand inhabitants.

Government House is a huge and imposing building, and in it is that famous Council Room, with the portraits of Hastings and others on its walls, where the welfare or fate of millions of souls has often hung in the balance. In the immediate neighbourhood, are the modern and majestic Law Courts, with towers and fretted roof. Behind, rises the dome of the Post Office, a noble building; and along the road called Chowringee, looking out upon the Maidan, or common, six miles in circumference, are the large houses, each within its gardens or "compound," that have won for the place the name "City of Palaces;" while the ravages of climate upon the health of European residents have

THE MAIDAN AT CALCUTTA.

suggested the parody, "City of Pale Faces." There are many statues and monuments about the Maidan, the creatures of official inspiration. To the west is the river, with its forest of masts; and Fort William, which covers some acres between the Maidan and the river to the south, is an imposing barrack with a very noble church. To the north runs the Chidpore Road, through the Black Town, full of natives and native shops, and parallel with it Cornwallis Street, noted for its charitable and educational institutions. These institutions all over Calcutta stand as the memorials of illustrious names. Here it was that Bishop Wilson toiled, and here stands his church, St. John's. Here, too, in a conspicuous position stands the Scotch Church, where the zealous and self-denying Dr. Duff laboured. In Cornwallis Square, is the College which he first founded, now in the hands of the Scotch Established Church; near it is the Free Church College, afterwards built by Dr. Duff, in which he taught for many years, and where a thousand young men and boys are daily assembled for religious and secular education. It is a giant building, and in the centre hall, where the school is wont to assemble to hear the Scriptures every morning, now stands a bust of that noble presence, placed there in loving remembrance of the founder. Not far off, on the banks of the river, is the Burning Ghaut, in the native quarter, where the process of cremation may be witnessed every day.

Early one morning, after the usual *Chota-Hasri*, or "little breakfast," served in the bedroom before rising, I was taken by a friend in a boat down the Hoogly to the Botanic Gardens, beyond the deserted-looking Bishop's College. The air on the river was cold and damp, reminding one a little of London fog, a strange contrast to the noonday heat of the city. A few boatmen were plying their craft lazily along. Opposite was the palace of the deposed monarch of Oude, who keeps tigers in his grounds. Landing at a wharf on the west bank, we at once entered the gardens, which cover three hundred acres, and happily combine the natural with the artificial; they contain beautiful specimens of the Mauritius, the talipot, the sago and other palms, a large variety of crotons, and, above all, a great banyan tree, with a girth of eighteen yards, whose branches and descending roots extend to a circumference of three hundred yards.

The same day we visited Kalighat, which gave its name to Calcutta, and is situated on the bank of an old bed of the Ganges, four miles south of the city. The legend is that when the corpse of the goddess Kali, wife of Siva, was cut in pieces by order of the gods, one of her fingers fell here, and a temple was raised in her honour. The present temple was built three hundred years ago, and renewed in 1809; its priests are called "Haldar," and amass great wealth from the daily offerings of pilgrims. There are many festivals, to which immense crowds resort, especially on the second day of the *Durja Puja*, the great Bengali religious festival in honour of the goddess, held at the autumnal equinox. The street off which the temple lies is full of shops for the sale of idol pictures, images and charms. When we arrived, sacrifices were being offered in the midst of an excited crowd. In an area before the temple stood the priest, and beside him the executioner, sword in hand. We saw three kids and two buffaloes sacrificed. The head of the victim is fastened in a wooden vice, its body is held up by the hind legs, and the sacrificer strikes with his sword. If the head is severed with one stroke, the victim is considered acceptable to the goddess, and its blood is collected by the priest, carried into the shrine, and sprinkled upon her huge projecting tongue. We could see in the distance the hideous idol within, its tongue streaming with blood. If the head of the animal is not severed with the first stroke, it is considered unacceptable, and is cast aside. The officiating Brahman, almost naked, with

BANYAN IN CALCUTTA BOTANIC GARDENS.

the sacred cord round his neck, was a fierce-looking, but very shrewd man. He could speak English. We found that he had been when a boy five years at the Bhowanipore Mission School, and that a near kinsman of his was a convert to Christianity and a missionary. Upon my saying, "How can you carry on these revolting rites? You know that they are vain, and a pretence," he replied, "Yes, I know it; but the people will have it, and I must get my living." The man evidently disbelieved in his heathenism, and might be a professor of Christianity if he saw it would pay. It was strange and saddening to see these bloody, exciting, and degrading rites amid a huge gathering of devotees within a few miles of English civilisation and fashion. Only a mile away is the large college and compound of the London Mission. Two miles nearer town stands the cathedral of St. Paul, in "the churchwarden Gothic style," with its library and statue of Bishop Heber. And in the evening the fashionables of Calcutta, pale and listless, might be seen rolling in gay equipages in lines three deep, across the Maidan, and by the shipping along the river-side, and gathering round the band in the Eden Gardens. In the temple area at Kalighat, around the shrine of Kali, you see Hindu caste and idolatry in all their proud and devout barbarism; the same day, at evening, in the Eden Gardens, around the band you may witness the pomp and vanity of Anglo-Indian caste, from the haughty Collector who lives upon the taxes, to the industrious tradesman who pays them. Brahman and Sudra you find alike in both assemblies; and it is not easy to decide which is the more unreasonable and inexcusable, the heathen or the official pride.

RELIGIOUS MENDICANT.

The Mohammedans of Calcutta have a large educational establishment, called the Madrisa, where the pupils are instructed in languages and Mohammedan law, and graduate at the Calcutta University. The new theistic sect called the Brahmo-somaj has a Mandir, or church, for the "Progressive Brahmos," as the party headed by K. C. Sen is called. They have normal and adult schools, and a small girls' school. The Hindu College, in College Square, is a handsome building of the Ionic order.

Starting one morning early by railway from Sealdah Station, we travelled about eighteen miles north to Samnuggur, where we were taken over a cotton factory, and found the rooms as airy as in Lancashire, though, of course, hotter. The workpeople looked healthy and content. The average wages per month are, for a girl, ten shillings; a woman, sixteen shillings; a man thirty-two shillings. The Hoogly, which flows close by, is deep and wide, and there is an interesting old temple with beautifully carved stone in the neighbourhood. The river view is very picturesque, commanding a reach of the river, teeming with rural beauty. Farther up are Hugli and Bandel, where is a monastery said to be the oldest in Bengal, dating from 1599. Returning to Barrackpore, on the same line, we drove through the park, a charming, quiet retreat, not unlike Kew Gardens, on the banks of the Hoogly, whither the Viceroy usually comes to spend the Sunday. The house commands a noble prospect six miles down the river. A short distance off is Lady Canning's tomb, which occupies a charming spot on the banks of the river. Her remains have long since been removed to England. The park contains many good trees, palms of various kinds, banyan trees, lovely pine-like casuarinas, and graceful bamboos. In the neighbourhood are the filtering-beds, through which the waters of the Ganges pass to supply Calcutta.

Immediately opposite to Barrackpore, on the west bank of the river, is Serampore, once a Danish settlement, thirteen miles from Calcutta, where are the famous Baptist College and the scenes of the labours of Carey, Marshman, and Ward. Carey landed at Calcutta in 1793, and after some struggles for subsistence set up a printing press. His colleagues came in 1797: and they would all have been reshipped by the authorities, had they not found refuge at Serampore, under the protection of the Danish flag. The college is a substantial building, with a noble staircase, and possesses a fine library, in which is an interesting collection of Bibles in Oriental languages, and some valuable manuscripts. One of Carey's, a polyglot dictionary of Sanscrit words with the corresponding word in six languages, is beautifully written, and shows the toil and perseverance of its author. The burial-

SERAMPORE COLLEGE.

ground is about half a mile distant, where lie the mortal remains of Carey, Ward, and Marshman. Carey's tomb has this inscription:

WILLIAM CAREY.

Born, 17th August, 1761;
Died, 9th June, 1834.

"A guilty, weak, and helpless worm,
On Thy kind arms I fall."

MARTYN'S HOME, ALDEEN, SERAMPORE.

The tombs of all three missionaries have domes, supported on pillars; but the ground has the air of neglect and decay, and the wall near Carey's tomb is broken down. We next drove to the Danish church in which Carey preached. It is now in the hands of the Establishment. Near the mission chapel a large jute factory has been erected. Not far off, on the river side, at Aldeen, stood the pagoda where another eminent missionary, Henry Martyn, took up his abode on his arrival in India in the year 1806, and where he spent many hours in learning Hindustani and translating portions of the Scriptures. It is a picturesque and interesting spot. He thus speaks of it in his journal: "The habitation assigned me by Mr. Brown, is a pagoda in his grounds, on the edge of the river. Thither I retired at night, and really felt something like superstitious dread at being in a place once inhabited, as it were, by devils; but yet felt disposed to be triumphantly joyful, that the temple where they were worshipped was become Christ's Oratory. I prayed out aloud to my God, and the echoes returned from the vaulted roof. Oh! may I so pray that the dome of heaven may resound! I like my dwelling much, it is so retired and free from noise; it has so many recesses and cells, that I can hardly find my way in and out." The building has in part been washed away by the river.

Serampore has a calm and cheerful aspect, with its clean shady roads. It is a pleasant suburban retreat, but factories are gaining ground, and the mission has the air of decay. Carey's Botanical Garden of six acres, which contained three thousand species of plants and trees, is now jungle, and has recently been sold for business purposes. There is a considerable silk manufacture here. It is sad to see the scenes of many years of Christian labour, and the fruits of missionary enterprise associated with revered names, thus on the decline. The headquarters of the mission, it should however be remembered, have been removed to Calcutta. Twelve miles farther on is the French settlement of Chandernagore, dating from 1688, pleasantly situated on the river side. It consists of a long row of white buildings interspersed with trees. But, as has been quaintly said, "it looks a little out at elbows, and has about it a shabby genteel sort of air."

ASSAM, with its capital Shillong, in the Khasi Hills, includes the fertile Brahmaputra valley, with its rich black soil. Its hills in the east contain limestone and coal beds, and tea is largely cultivated on their lower slopes. The population is four millions, chiefly Hindus and Mohammedans. All depend for their livelihood upon agriculture, and the staple crop is rice. The climate is very humid, and fogs often rise from the river.

DARJEELING, "Holy Spot," as the word signifies, the hill station nearest to Calcutta, lies north about four hundred miles. The Eastern Bengal Railway runs in a northerly direction for about a hundred miles over the plains of Bengal, in about five hours, to Damookdea on the Ganges. It passes near Krishnuggur, a town of forty thousand inhabitants, where the Church Mission has its headquarters for the district; and thirty miles west is Plassey, where Clive won, in 1757, the memorable victory from which virtually dates the British supremacy in North India. A large steam ferry conveyed us across the Ganges from Damookdea in forty minutes. It is a perilous passage, owing to the strong current and the shoals; two men were taking soundings one on each side the vessel, all the way across. At Sara Ghat, we again entered the train, and travelled all night, two hundred miles, stopping at many stations, till we reached the temporary terminus, Silliguri, at about 10 A.M. Here, with much difficulty, and after some hours' delay, we obtained wretched ponies to take us on to Kursiong, half-way to Darjeeling; but our ponies travelled so slowly across the Serai, or swamp of low lying jungle, the seat of malarious fever, which forms a deadly belt along the foot of the hills across the north of India, separating the Himalayas, that darkness came on before we began to ascend, and we rode in faith along the road, which at the time was undergoing repair, till we reached the Dak Bungalow of Chambattie, where we put up for the night.

ON THE WAY TO THE HIMÂLAYAS.

The Dak Bungalow is an Inn or Rest House, provided by Government for travellers, one-storied, with verandas, often perched on a knoll; with scanty furniture and scantier fare. It is in charge of a native called a *Khansamah*, who locks it up when empty, and appears on the ground to open it when you call. A tariff of prices, very moderate, a list of rules, a list of articles provided, and a carefully-drawn map of the district, hang on the walls. After some delay we got candles and chocolate and bread; but it was too late to procure the usual repast of roast fowl, or "sudden death," as this dish is called in the East, the creature being usually killed and dressed within half-an-hour of your arrival. We turned in after giving directions to the khansamah to look after our ponies, and to prepare an early

KINCHINJUNGA, FROM DARJEELING.

morning meal. The silence of the hills was impressive; here and there a firefly, here and there, across the valley, or through the trees, the twinkle of the light in a native hut.

At daybreak next morning we were again in the saddle, and rode ten miles over lovely hills with wooded sides and varied ravines, clad in forest and brushwood to Kursiong. The views were fine, and the verdure beautiful. The air was delightfully clear and cool, and peasants of the native tribes were passing to their work along the mountain paths. Kursiong is four thousand six hundred feet above the sea, a village perched on the ridge of a hill; and here we had our first sight of the Himâlayas. Kinchinjunga, the second highest of the range, twenty-eight thousand feet, was full in view, though sixty miles away. The sight was grand and impressive. The air

TRAVELLER'S BUNGALOW.

became more keen and bracing, and after the refreshment of breakfast in a comfortable inn, we mounted fresh ponies and started on the remaining twenty miles. The road is lovely in the extreme, skirting the flanks and rounding the spurs of the mountains, carried by bridges over deep ravines with roaring torrents, and adorned with luxuriant tropical vegetation, splendid orchids, graceful tree-ferns, flowering creepers and noble trees. After crossing the ridge called "the Saddle," we came through the barracks used as a convalescent depôt, and rode on to the delightfully placed lodgings which we had beforehand engaged, distant just fifteen minutes' walk from the Observatory Hill and the Mall, and with the sublime snows towering high before us;—a spot much frequented by Calcutta officials during the hot season.

At sunrise on Sunday morning I walked round the Mall and up to the Observatory, which commands a full view of the stupendous scenery. Never did I understand so fully the force of the apostle's expression, "depth and height," as now that I had before me the giant mountains, and looked down into the depths, deeper and deeper still, six thousand feet, into the forest-clad ravine of the Great Ranjit river, and then slowly raised my eyes higher and higher through the successive ridges of foliage and rocks, till they reached the eternal snows, and still far up and up to the peaks soaring into the sky. From the lowest point which the eye can reach in the Ranjit valley to the highest peak of Kinchinjunga, the vertical height is not less than five miles —such a thickness of the earth's crust being probably nowhere else visible on the earth's surface. More than twelve peaks can be counted which rise above twenty thousand feet. The air was cold and bracing, the grass was crisp and white with frost; the sun shot his rays across in dazzling splendour, and in the stillness and brightness of the scene one felt as if transported to another world. After morning service in the little English church, I went down to the square bazaar or market-place, which is crowded on Sundays with strange nationalities. Here were the old aborigines, the LEPCHAS, with Mongolian type of face, oblique eyes, high cheek-bones, clad in striped cotton garments; the men with pigtails like the Chinese, the women with nose-rings and large silver ornaments, some with strings of rupees. They are a small, plain, but powerful-looking race, inured to hardship, nomadic, but amiable. Their besetting sin is gambling. They are a merry and careless people, with but little thought of the morrow. They are very fond of quoits, using pieces of slate for the purpose, which they throw with great dexterity. They always wear a long knife, curved like a sickle and stuck in the girdle, which serves them to fell trees, skin animals, build huts, pare their nails, sever their food, and even pick their

HIMÂLAYA HILL GIRL.

TEMPLE AND SACRED TANK, NEPAL.

teeth. Rice is their staple food. Their language is a Thebetan dialect, and their religion a corrupt Buddhism.

Here, too, in large numbers, were the Bhooteas, tall and robust, sturdy, flat-faced people, weather-beaten, with broad mouths and flat noses; their complexion whitish yellow, but encrusted with dirt, and tar, and smoke. They seldom wash. They are dressed in loose blankets girt about the waist with a leather belt, in which they place their brass pipes, their long knives, chopsticks, tinder-box, tobacco-pouch and tweezers, with which they pluck away all trace of beard. They wear stout woven boots—boot and stocking in one. The women have their faces tarred, and their hair is plaited in two tails, the neck loaded with strings of coral and amber, large heavy, round earrings, dragging down the lobe of the ear. They are always spinning. The Bhooteas are Buddhists, and believe in the efficacy of praying-machines. When crossing mountains they hang little scraps of rag on the bushes, as a prayer for safety, and place grains of rice along the hillside to propitiate evil spirits. They bury their dead on the mountains, raising cairns over them.

Here, again, one might see the light and agile Nepalese, with intelligent and pleasing countenances, active and enduring, and brave to a degree, as the Nepal war (1816) witnesses. Their secluded valleys are rich in forest and minerals, and on the frontier indigo is largely grown. Their dogs are yellow-fanged, wolf-like, fierce, surly creatures, but invaluable watch-dogs. Nepal proper is a small valley twelve miles by nine at the foot of this part of the Himâlayan range, but the country extends west from Sikkim to Kumaon. The ruling race are called Ghûrkas. Here Buddhism and Vaishnavism are found side by side. The temples are of wood, and remind one of those of Japan. The temple of Mahadeva at Patan presents both styles of architecture, the Hindu and the Thibetan or Turanian side by side. The capital of Nepal is Khatmandu, and contains a beautiful temple in the Chinese style. The view of the Himâlayas to the north-east is very grand. The ragged Lama mendicant is also to be met with, and Sherbas and Thibetan beggars, jovial, but easily excited. Intermingled with these native mountain tribes were stolid Chinamen, proud Mahommedans, and graceful Hindus. In the midst of the bustle and bartering, the missionary had his open room, or shed, into which the people came to hear hymn, or prayer, or Scripture. In the Bhootea village there is a small, dirty Buddhist temple called Bhootea Bustee. The Lamas, or priests, are also of a low type, unctuous, sly, insolent. They sell praying-machines (Mani), and use them in their worship, continually turning them round. Indeed, you enter the temple between two huge cylinders, like pillars, two feet in diameter and six feet high, which are gigantic praying machines, turned by means of a winch. Here we met many Thibetans returning to their country with heavy burdens.

Rising one morning while it was yet dark and starlight, we mounted our ponies, and, with guides, started for the ascent of the SINCHAL MOUNTAIN (eight thousand three hundred feet), six miles from *Darjeeling*. *Riding* through the military sanatorium to "the Saddle," or *Johr Bungalow*, we

PALACE AND TEMPLE, KHATMANDU, NEPAL.

began the ascent up a steep winding track through the jungle, and after an hour's climb reached the Chimneys—the ruins of the first military station—perched upon a ridge, or shoulder of Sinchal, where Kinchinjunga and its neighbour peaks burst on our view, kindled with the rays of the rising sun. The air was perfectly clear, and the sky cloudless. Here we dismounted, and scrambled through brushwood and snow to the summit, which is specially celebrated, because of the glorious prospect it commands—the sweep of the Himâlayan range, including Everest itself, the presiding monarch of them all, the highest mountain in the world. There he rose to our view, of sugar-loaf shape, far off, but clear cut against the sky. The entire range "Pelion on Ossa piled," was now before us as far as the eye could reach in a clear atmosphere and a cloudless sky. It was like looking from a Pisgah across the valleys and over mountains to a new and loftier country. Here one is overwhelmed with the majesty of Nature and the power of the Almighty. The deep blue sky, the pure white snows, the clear-cut precipices, the dark, shady ravines, the dense primeval forests, all impress the spectator with the presence of God. Having filled the eye and mind with the sublimity of a prospect never to be forgotten during two hours spent on that green, but now frost-whitened mountain, we reluctantly descended to the shoulder where our ponies were, and returned thankful and exultant that we had been so favoured in the weather; for these grandeurs are often enveloped in mist or cloud for days together. The annual average rainfall at Darjeeling is nine feet eight inches—one hundred and sixteen inches—June to September being the wettest months.

DANDY TRAVELLING, HIMÂLAYAS.

The descent from Darjeeling to the Ranjit river, which separates it from the Himalayan range, is six thousand feet in eleven miles, and the river is crossed by one of those cane bridges which are peculiar to this part of the world. The main chains supporting the bridge are branches of trees, and rattan canes; the sides are of split canes, hanging from each main chain, two feet apart. Into these loops the foot-path is laid, composed of three bamboos, the thickness of a man's arm, laid side by side, the section of the bridge resembling the letter V, in the angle or base of which the traveller finds footing. The piers of these bridges are generally two convenient trees through whose branches the main chains are passed and pegged into the ground beyond. Only one traveller can pass over at a time, and the spring

BRIDGE OVER THE RANJIT RIVER, DARJEELING.

and oscillation are considerable, but strong bamboos are placed underneath and connected with the main chains by split rattan ropes to prevent the bridge from collapsing with the weight.

At the lower edge of the great forest which clothes the Sinchal lies a botanical garden, lonely and lovely, the Rungaroon Garden, where we found roses, scarlet geraniums, verbenas, and many English plants and flowers in the midst of tropical luxuriance. The garden is to be devoted to such indigenous plants, epiphytes, orchids, gingers, etc., as are not likely to thrive in the moister and more shady forest sections. The path leading to this spot is rich in forest beauty. Beyond are some of the tea and cinchona plantations for which Darjeeling is famous, and which, as the slopes are cleared, mar in some degree the beauty of the nearer hills. The tea gardens are laid out in the most unromantic fashion, acre upon acre planted with straight rows of bushes two feet high with small glazed dark green leaves, and in the centre the manager's bungalow flanked by long ranges of low buildings, where the process of drying, sorting and packing is carried on. The Bhootea coolies, both men and women, may be seen carrying chests of immense weight up the steepest hills. They leave the railway porters of England far behind. A story is told that one of these sturdy women actually brought up a grand piano on her back from Kursiong to the station. The work on the plantations is not so laborious. It consists mainly in deep hoeing between the lines of trees as weeds appear, and careful hand weeding. In November of the third year, when the plant is four feet high, it is pruned down to twenty inches, that the young leaves may be plucked easily; and six weeks afterwards, when the tea plant is said to "flush," or throw out new shoots six inches high, the picking is repeated, and so on at intervals of twenty days for eight months. Tea can be made only of these young and tender leaves, and the plucking requires gentle touch, women and children being employed. For sorting, rolling, drying, etc., machinery is generally used.

The cinchona (quinine) plantations in the Darjeeling district cover nearly two thousand acres, stocked with about three million cinchona trees. The quinine comes from the bark. Quinidine, or cinchonidine, chiefly from the red cinchona, is a good substitute for quinine. It is produced in large quantities, and is obtainable at a much more moderate cost.

Language cannot describe the glory of the Himâlayas seen from Darjeeling lit up by the rays of the setting sun. From the Observatory more than twelve peaks can be counted, which rise above twenty thousand feet, and none are below fifteen thousand. Against the azure sky, in an atmosphere far clearer than we ever see in England, the snowy range reflects the colours of the sunset, ever changing and deepening in richness from bright yellow to pink, from pink to crimson, and long after the sun has set to us. Well may one writer speak of the view as "something to be treasured as one of the most noteworthy moments of his life;" and another of "the deep happiness of a sojourn in this enchanted land, sentinelled by the ever-lasting mountains." And the contrast from these "abodes of snow," to the luxuriant tropical vegetation surrounding us on every hand, clothing the richly-wooded hills through which we drive, is hardly less striking and impressive.

The natives are loth to stir early, for they feel the morning cold, and are ill prepared against it as to clothing; but with the Himâlayas now bright with the rising sun we succeeded in starting by Tonga Dâk (a sort of dog-cart) at 8 A.M., reaching Kursiong at 11 A.M. and Sillijuri in time for the evening train. The transition as we drove along from snow and frost to firs and oaks, then to rhododendrons, indiarubber-trees, tree-ferns of immense size, golden ferns with stems three feet high, and wondrous orchids, white,

RAILWAY TRAVELLING.

yellow, and purple, banks studded with stag-moss and yellow calceolarias, scented magnolia and magnificent bamboos—gives an exhilaration and excitement not to be had to the same extent in any other part of the world.

The East Indian Railway runs north-west from Calcutta up the Ganges valley nine hundred and fifty-four miles to Delhi; and at Delhi it meets the Scinde Punjab and Indus Valley State Railways, which complete the iron road by Lahore away still northward to Peshawar, and southwards to Karâchi, that important and rising port at the mouth of the Indus one thousand one hundred and sixty-nine miles from Delhi. Thus the railway journey across India from Calcutta to Karâchi is two thousand one hundred and twenty-three miles, and from Calcutta to Bombay, branching south from Allahabad, is fourteen hundred and nine miles. The river Ganges with its tributaries drains an area of three hundred and ninety thousand square miles, including the Lower Provinces of Bengal, the North-West Provinces and Oude. Here the Aryan race, entering from the north-west, attained their full strength and development. Hindi, Hindustani, or Bengali is their language, with the written character called

GRAIN SELLERS.

Nagari, resembling the ancient Sanscrit. The population is estimated at sixty millions. Their life is for the most part a struggle for existence by the tillage of the soil—rice, plantains, cocoanuts, and the cultivation of indigo, hemp, cotton and the opium poppy. The land is not, as in England, parcelled out into farms. There are wealthy proprietors, who hold large tracts by grant, purchase, or hereditary succession ; but the tenants are literally children of the soil. Wherever a village nestles among its plantains or mango groves, the land is parcelled out among the villagers. The villagers or immediate cultivators of soil are called *ryots*. The land-owners are called *zamindars*.

A large proprietor does not reckon up his farms, but he counts his villages. Often between the zamindars and the ryots there are middle-men or lease-holders (*patnidars*), who are sometimes indigo planters. Having got the village on lease, you summon the tenants, show them their rent account, and get them to agree to cultivate a certain percentage of the land in indigo. The compact being made, the ryots are your slaves for ever. The sowing of every year goes to pay the debt of the last, and the debt must be paid off by so many bundles of the indigo plant. The planter's bungalow is a fine-looking house, with an immense compound. In front of it is the factory, and at some distance miserable huts in which the coolies live.[1] In the

BULLOCK CARRIAGE.

cultivation of the land bullocks are used for draught and carriage. The Bengal plough is much the same as the Greek or Roman one. "The English have no idea," says Sir J. B. Phear, "of the extreme poverty of the bulk of the Bengal population. Seven rupees a month will support a whole family. Food is the principal item, and probably one rupee eight annas a month will suffice to feed an adult man, and twelve annas a woman." Yet the salt tax alone averages annually a hundred and twelve annas per head upon the entire population. "Famine," says another experienced writer, "is the horizon of the Indian villager; insufficient food is the

[1] Any one who would learn what Indian village life is, should read *Bengal Peasant Life*, by the Rev. L. B. Day; and *The Aryan Village*, by Sir J. B. Phear

foreground. And this is the more extraordinary, since the villager is surrounded by a dreamland of plenty. Everywhere you see fields flooded deep with millet and wheat. The village and its old trees have to climb on to a knoll to keep their feet out of the glorious poppy and the luscious sugar-cane. Sumptuous cream-coloured bullocks move sleepily about with an air of luxurious sloth. Everything is steeped in repose. The bees murmur their idylls among the flowers; the doves moan their amorous complaints from the shady leafage of pipal trees; out of the cool recesses of wells the idle cooing of the pigeons ascends into the summer-laden air; the rainbow-fed chameleon slumbers on the branch; the enamelled beetle on the leaf; the little fish is in the sparkling depths below; the radiant kingfisher, tremulous as sunlight, in mid-air; and the peacock with furled glories, on the temple tower of the silent gods. Amid this easeful and luscious splendour the villager labours and starves. While he has to maintain the glorious phantasmagoria of an imperial policy, while he has to support legions of scarlet soldiers, golden cuprassies, purple politicals, and green commissions, he must remain the hunger-stricken, over-driven phantom that he is."[1] What with income tax, licence tax, succession tax, salt tax, feast tax, and fast tax, his hookah—his "hubble-bubble," so called from the gurgling noise of the water inside the cocoanut-shell—is his only solace amid the privations of his wretched life. When he would protest, he dies of famine; this is his revenge.

THUGS.

[1] *Twenty-one Days in India*, by G. A. Mackay.

Through this vast district the railroad now wends its way. Before it came along the great trunk road travellers were often attacked, robbed, and even murdered in the days of Thug notoriety. The Thugs, who abounded chiefly in the forests, were fanatics who made highway robbery part of their religion, and declared that their victims were sacrifices to the goddess Kali. Disguised as peaceful travellers, they would first engage in simple and friendly greeting, looking gentle and unassuming, and then suddenly they would throw the handkerchief noose round the neck of the wayfarer, strangle him in a moment, and rifle him of all he possessed. Sometimes a girl appeared sitting at the wayside weeping. The traveller, in pity, might stop to speak to her; but if so he was doomed. She soon had the noose round his throat, and strangled him on the spot. Since 1830 Thuggism has been suppressed, but the instinct possesses the thieves still, and the sight of the noose will cause the calm features to blaze with fury. In the school of industry at Jabalpur, some aged Thugs, proud of their race and profession, may still be seen. A visitor anxious to understand their mode of strangling, submitted his neck to be operated upon, but at the great risk of his life; for with the kindling instinct of the Thug, the illustration threatened in another moment to become a reality. Datura poisoning is still practised by the same class of people. An old man and his son were lately poisoned for the sake of a new blanket by a gang of Thugs. The railroad now conveys us in ease and security over these vast plains. About one hundred and twenty miles from Calcutta we pass through Ranigunge, where there is the largest and most important coalfield in India. The miners are Bhowries and Sontals, low of stature, and great toilers, the former using the pick, the latter only the crowbar in getting the coal. The mines are not deep, and they are free from firedamp. In this district is Parasnath, the highest peak in Bengal proper, four thousand six hundred feet above the sea. It is a place of great sanctity to the Jains, who make yearly pilgrimages hither, and who strongly opposed the sanatorium for sick soldiers now erected on it. The mountain commands a grand panorama of the surrounding country, with its winding rivers and its wooded hills. The Sontals have made their way north to Raj Mahal, where by industry they have established themselves. Their villages are quite distinct and separate from those occupied by Hindus.

The chord line carries us between Chotia Nagpur on the south, and Behar on the north. Chotia Nagpur is a mountainous province inhabited chiefly by Dravidian tribes, the Kols and Oraons, among whom the Lutheran missionaries laboured successfully for many years. It is a succession of high tablelands called *Pats*, three thousand feet above the sea. In Behar we have the Patna district, which is famous for its rice, and the Gaya district, famous for its Buddhist remains. Behar, indeed, is the cradle of Buddhism, and the name is only a corruption of *Vihara*, a cave, or temple. Near Gaya is the site of the famous Bo-Tree, under which Gautama Buddha taught;

and the Elephant Rock, on which he sat with his disciples, is still pointed out. Here it was that Gautama learnt that the path to salvation lay not in penance and self-torture, but in preaching a higher life to his fellow-men. Here he became "the Buddha," the Enlightened, and began a ministry of love that lasted till his death at the age of eighty. In front of the Bo-Tree is the Buddh Gaya Temple, dating from the seventh century, and the Buddh Gaya rails are supposed to be the oldest Hindu sculptures hitherto found. There are several groups of cave temples, more or less ruined, in the neighbourhood, and bearing date from Asoka, B.C. 250.

TRAVELLING WAGGONS.

Hindu pilgrims come hither to adore the footprint of Vishnu on a rock. Shraddhas, *i.e.*, offerings in honour of departed relatives, are performed here at the Vishnu-pada temple, situated on one of the ridges, and built of black stone with a lofty dome and golden pinnacle. Various offerings are placed by the pilgrims round the footprint, the object being to help the progress of the souls of ancestors departed to heaven, and the time occupied in the rites being at least eight days.

The loop line runs through Behar and brings us through Colgong, where several rocky islands of granite interrupt the channel of the Ganges; the chief of these, Divinath, a sacred island, is crowned with a Hindu temple.

Several idols are carved on the rocks, and in places there are wedge-marks, showing that monoliths have been split off. These are the only rocks that interrupt the course of the Ganges for a thousand miles. The boats on the Ganges used for the conveyance of grain, cotton, etc., float down the stream at the rate of four miles an hour; and when ascending they hoist a sail, and are carried up by the south wind which habitually blows. The small English steamers on the river had originally the ordinary rudder; but it was found necessary to adopt the large broad helm which the native boats have had from time immemorial, as the only shape which would act in the strong current.

COLGONG ROCKS, GANGES.

HINDU TEMPLES, BENARES.

THE NORTH-WEST PROVINCES AND OUDE.

MOHAMMEDAN SCHOOL, ALLAHABAD.

THE NORTH-WEST PROVINCES AND OUDE.

BENARES, THE HOLY CITY—THE MUTINY CITIES: LUCKNOW AND CAWNPORE—THE MOHAMMEDAN CITIES: AGRA AND ALLAHABAD.

How pleasant, after a long wearisome railway journey of five hundred miles across the plains of Bengal, on reaching the terminus opposite the great stronghold of heathenism, Benares, the sacred city of the Hindus, with the mighty Ganges flowing between, to find Christians and friends waiting to receive you. So was it with us when on our arrival, a *sayce*, or footman, from the mission conducted us across the bridge of boats and through the city four miles to the European settlement and to our hotel; and when presently that eminent oriental scholar and missionary, the Rev. M. A. Sherring, whose premature death has since been announced, came to welcome and to guide us in our plans for sightseeing. Having crossed the Ganges, we were now in the North-West Provinces, and in the headquarters of idolatry in India. What Jerusalem is to the Jew, what Rome is to the Latin, what Mecca is to the Mohammedan,

Benares is to the Hindu. It contains fourteen hundred Hindu temples, idols innumerable, and twenty thousand Brahmans. Like Paul at Athens, the Christian's spirit is moved within him as he sees the city wholly given to idolatry. Troops of pilgrims are continually thronging its streets, and swarming up and down its *ghats*, or flights of steps leading down to the Ganges, along which the city stretches for three miles, rising gracefully upon the solitary cliff, up the face of which it is built tier upon tier.

A VISHNUVITE FAKÍR.

In Benares we see what Hinduism practically is. Students of the *Vedas* may restrict the term Brahmanism "to the purely pantheistic and not necessarily idolatrous system evolved by the Brahmans out of the partly monotheistic, partly polytheistic, partly pantheistic religion," expressed in those sacred songs. But it is the polytheistic element which has become its life and soul, embodied as this is in the Hinduism of India. Hinduism is, in fact, idolatry of the basest kind, the worship of *Vishnu* the preserver, and *Siva* the destroyer, represented by numberless idols and symbols of the most revolting character. Here in the North-West Provinces, and above all in Benares, Hinduism has acquired a stony compactness, and a solidity almost impenetrable. Here Brahmanism and caste hold sway. The Hindustani, stalwart, tall, strong-limbed, independent, solid, proudly rests on his good breed, good blood, and the associations of antiquity. He adores the social hierarchy; and all the great events of life, births, marriages, deaths, occupations, professions, are interlaced and enchained with the overgrown fabric of his idolatry. And Benares is the centre of all this. It is a very ancient city, and is frequently alluded to in early Sanscrit literature. For the sanctity of its inhabitants, of its temples and reservoirs, of its wells and streams, Benares has been famed for thousands of years. Here, to quote the high authority of the lamented Rev. M. A. Sherring, "idolatry is a charm, a fascination, to the Hindu. It is, so to speak, the air he breathes. It is the food of his soul. He is subdued, enslaved, befooled by it. The nature of the Hindu partakes of the supposed nature of the gods whom he worships. And what is that nature? According to the traditions handed about amongst the natives, and constantly dwelt upon in their conversation, and referred to in their popular songs—which perhaps would be sufficient proof—yet more especially according to the numberless statements and narratives found in their sacred writings, on which these traditions are based, it is, in many instances, vile and abominable to the last degree. Idolatry is a word denoting all that is wicked in imagination and impure in practice. Idolatry is a demon—an incarnation of all evil—but nevertheless as bewitching and seductive as a Siren. It ensnares the depraved heart, coils around it like a serpent, transfixes it with its deadly fangs, and finally stings it to death." This is the testimony of a Sanscrit scholar who knew the Vedas well, and who lived thirty years among the Hindus, at the headquarters of Hinduism.

One Sunday morning at seven, we drove outside the city to the Church Mission compound, and as we approached saw the native children of the girls' and orphans' schools walking in procession into church, all neatly dressed, and in excellent order, so that you might imagine you were not in Benares, but in some English country parish. The bell was tolling for service, and entering we found a goodly gathering of Hindus. The service was read and the sermon preached in the native language. The houses of the missionaries are within the large compound, which looked refreshingly green and shaded with trees. Afterwards, at the London Mission compound, which is more within the city, we found a small native congregation. Missions have been prosecuted here now for sixty years by various societies; but little perceptible impression has been made upon the citadel of heathenism. A faithful witnessing for JESUS is maintained, but the converts are few. Conversions belong to God; and nothing so tests and testifies the strength of the labourer's faith and zeal and love as persevering labour without apparent results. During the week I visited the London Missionary College, where four hundred native young men and boys are educated. And as I went from class-room to class-room, filled with scholars learning not only their native Hindustani, but Sanscrit, Arabic, and English, as well as arithmetic, mathematics, chemistry; as I sat in the head-master's room—Mr. Sherring's—and found him at work teaching the Scriptures to a class of intelligent-looking young men, all natives; as I spoke to them in English, and heard their shrewd questions and answers, I felt that certainly a powerful influence here is working and multiplying, shedding light upon many minds, awakening intellectual freedom, and producing a moral and religious life, before which idolatry must eventually totter and fall.

Taking time by the forelock, and gladly seizing the cool of early morning, we started next day under the Rev. M. A. Sherring's conduct, to see the sights. And first we visited the mansion of the Maharajah of Vizianagram, furnished in European style, and showing the inroads of Western civilisation. Not far from this is the Durga Temple, at the southern extremity of the city. Bloody sacrifices are offered to the goddess Durga (or Kali) in front of her shrine every Tuesday. The temple swarms with reddish-brown monkeys in every nook, along every wall, and about the streets and bazaars. These monkeys are all regarded as living deities, gods and goddesses, and of greater sanctity far than the poor people living round about who are annoyed by them. Hinduism, instead of tracing men to monkeys like Darwinism, raises monkeys to be gods, a step higher than men. Proceeding to the Dasasamed Ghât, we left our carriage and ascended the Man-Mandil Observatory, containing several large astronomical instruments erected by the Rajah Say Singh in 1693. Here there is a beautifully-carved oriel window, commanding a fine view of the river. The Rajah Si Bahadur received us with politeness. Close by is the temple of the rain god, supposed to exercise power over the clouds in procuring rain. The idol is placed in a cistern low down in the centre of the temple, and kept drenched with water. The Nepalese temple, rising from the banks of the Ganges near the Man-Mandil Ghât, is a strikingly picturesque object, and is now the only Buddhist temple in Benares.

The Dasasamed Ghât is one of the five celebrated places of pilgrimage in Benares. Here we saw one of those religious devotees called *Fakîrs*, who live upon charity, and obtain a reputation for sanctity by abstinence, retaining the body in one position, and imposing severe penances upon themselves. They suffer their hair to grow in long shaggy locks, sometimes reaching to the ground, and their austerities are regarded with reverence and admiration. At the Burning Ghât, whither a boat conveyed us, there lay a corpse with wood piled round it, prepared for cremation, and another funeral pile, with its smouldering embers just burnt out. Funeral rites are continually going on here; for many come to Benares as the goal of their hope and life on purpose to die. Several pairs of short slabs set up on end, called *suttee*, mark the spots where widows have been burnt alive on the pyre of their husbands. The word *suttee* means "chaste or faithful woman." The custom was prohibited by the government in 1829; but these spots are still the objects of worship.

Our boat conveyed us next to the steps dividing the city along the river into two equal portions and leading up to the famous WELL OF SALVATION. At the top this well is twenty yards long and ten wide, and flights of steps slope down the four sides like a pyramid reversed to a narrow trough of water at the bottom in which devotees were standing, washing face and head, and sipping the fœtid water from their hands. It is believed that this well, filled with the sweat of Vishnu, infallibly washes away all sin. The water is disgustingly dirty, as though it held in solution the sins it washed away. Near this well is the temple of Ganesh, the god of wisdom, represented as a figure painted red, with three eyes and an elephant's trunk, over which a cloth is drawn, like that which a barber wraps about a man before shaving him. At the feet of the god is the figure of a rat, the animal on which he is supposed to ride. Passing the Rajah of Nagpore's Ghât, where the massive masonry has given way, we saw swarms of people streaming down the several stairs and along the bathing platforms as we sailed slowly past; and very picturesque they looked, some bathing, some praying, some dressing, and multitudes going up and coming down. Leaving the boat at the needle-like minarets which strike the eye in every view of Benares, and appear in almost every photograph, we climbed first the long, broad flight of steps, and then the narrow winding staircase inside the minaret, and obtained from the summit (three hundred feet above the river) a wide view of the city and the surrounding country. The mosque, with its strong and deep foundations, and its exquisitely graceful minarets, was built by Aurangzeb, a bigot and a persecutor, the last, the most cruel, intolerant, and hated of the Moguls, 1658–1707. He imprisoned his father, Sháh Jahán, murdered his brothers, imposed the *Jiziah*, a religious tax, on every one not Mohammedan, destroyed Hindu temples, and built mosques out of the materials,

INDIAN FAKÍR.

in particular, this at Benares, still the most conspicuous object, towering over all the temples of Brahmanism.

Traversing the narrow streets on foot, the only way in which they can be traversed, for nearly a mile, we next visited the famous temple of the police deity of the city (*kotwal*), symbolised by a huge truncheon of stone, called *dandpan*, four feet high, which is worshipped by many people every

BENARES.

week. In front of it priests with rods of peacock feathers were inflicting very gentle vicarious punishment upon the worshippers. Walking through the quarter of the city devoted to the manufacture of Benares brasswork (where you see boys hammering the patterns with a small punch) we reached the Golden Temple, dedicated to the god Bisheshwar, or Siva, whose image is the *lingam*, a plain conical stone set on end. This is the reigning deity of Benares, and this is its chief temple in the city. As you approach it from the north you pass through a court where is a large collection of images chiefly *linga*, male and female emblems. They are from the ruins of the older temple which Aurangzeb destroyed. They are all objects of worship and bear marks of adoration—garlands of flowers, oil and paint. Before the central *lingam* you see the Hindu worshippers prostrating themselves; and this worship is the centre and culmination of Brahmanism in India. This temple, like all the Benâres temples, is of a mean and dirty aspect, but it is surmounted by a gilded tower and dome glittering in the sun fifty feet high. Adjoining is the "Well of Knowledge," giving forth a loathsome stench. The spectator turns away from all with pain, horror, and disgust.

The great sight of Benares is, after all, its river front in the early morning, when the rays of sunrise flood the city with brightness, and its inhabitants bathe in their sacred river. Seated on the deck of a large river boat, called a *dingee*, we floated slowly along with the lazy tide watching the panorama of human life and devotion. Men, women and children of all ages were crowding the ghâts and performing their ablutions in the yellow flood, as a daily act of refreshment, of purification, and of religion; worshipping the river, basking in the sun, bottling up vessels of the sacred water for purifying purposes at home, and then going to the priests to have painted on their shining foreheads the distinctive marks of their caste. Above the motley crowd rose the towering temples and the mosques, tinted with red or burnished with gold. The Hindus are a devout and religious people, and their zeal and earnestness in what is false, may teach a lesson to those who know the true.

Benares is not only the headquarters of Brahmanism, it is the cradle of Buddhism. After six years' asceticism and solitude at Gaya, Gautama Buddha, B.C. 590, having experienced his temptation and his enlightenment under the Bo-tree, made his way to Benares, affirming, "I am going to that city, to give light to those enshrouded in darkness, and to open the gates of immortality to men." The place where he taught, once called the Deer Park, now Sarnath, lies four miles north-west of the city, and is marked by a large collection of Buddhist remains. Here are two large *Stupas* or Topes, sacred octagonal towers, built by King Asoka 250 B.C., separated about half a mile from each other, but connected by ruins of walls and foundations of buildings lately exhumed and heaps of thickly scattered bricks. The Buddhist *Stupa*, or Tope, is in shape and appearance like an enormous bee-hive, raised hundreds of feet in height, beautifully ornamented, and surrounded by a massive stone rail. It was raised usually as a memorial of some event, or as a relic-shrine. This at Benares, called Dhamek, is a solid round tower, ninety-three feet in diameter at base, one hundred and twenty-eight feet in height. The lower part is built entirely of stone, the upper part of large bricks. The lower part has eight projecting faces with niches to receive a statue. The eight statues have disappeared, but they probably represented Buddha the preacher, life size with uplifted hand. The sides are richly decorated with a profusion of flowering foliage,

TOPE AT SARNATH.

below which the middle band is formed of various geometric figures deeply cut. The upper band is a scroll of the lotus plant with leaves and buds; the lower band is similar but with full-blown flowers. In the middle of the lower ornamentation there is a human figure seated on a lotus flower, and holding two branches of the lotus in his hands. On each side of him there are three lotus flowers, of which the four nearer ones support pairs of sacred geese, while the two farther ones carry only single birds. Over the nearest pair of geese on the right hand of the figure there is a frog. The attitudes of the birds are all good, and even that of the human figure is easy, although formal. The lotus scroll is very rich and beautiful. The breadth of each of the eight faces is thirty-six feet six inches.

We entered a passage at the base of the tower which leads right

SCULPTURE ON TOPE AT SARNATH.

through. In the centre there is a shaft open to the top. To the west of the tower are the remains of a great hospital and of an old Buddhist monastery. A second tope surmounted by a tower, called Lori's Leap, consists of a mound of solid brickwork seventy-four feet high. The tower above it is an octagonal building erected (1531) to commemorate the ascent of the mound on which it stands by the Emperor Humayun.

The last votaries of Buddha were driven from India in the twelfth century. Numbers of images, concealed by the departing monks, are found buried near Sarnath; and heaps of ashes scattered amid the ruins show that the monasteries were destroyed by fire. Thus it took several centuries to extirpate Buddhism from India.

Lucknow, the capital of Oudh, a State which is now included with the North-West Provinces, is a city of three hundred thousand inhabitants, situated on the banks of the river Gumti, the Oudh tributary of the Ganges. At first sight it impresses the visitor as a most beautiful city, containing a galaxy of majestic buildings of dazzling whiteness, crowned with domes of burnished gold and scores of minarets. But a nearer view destroys the illusion. The white colour of the buildings is not marble, it is simply wash, the material for the most part is not stone but stucco, and the domes are mere shells of wood. Still the distances in the city are great, the roads admirable and planted with trees, and the gardens and parks are for beauty and extent unsurpassed in any city in India. The architecture of Lucknow is for the most part tawdry and unsubstantial; the natural loveliness of the city's surroundings, with its well-wooded parks and charming flower gardens, is delightful. We first drove to the Dilkusa Palace, in a beautiful park stocked with deer, the head-quarters of Sir Colin Campbell's force during the Mutiny of 1857. Then to the Martinière, a strange fantastic building almost as imposing as a stucco Versailles. It was built and endowed by a Frenchman, Claude Martin, who came to India as a private soldier, and died a general and a millionaire. It was originally intended as a palace, but before it was finished the wealthy builder endowed it as a school—a happy change; and the spacious state-rooms are filled with little red beds, each child having one of his own. In front is a huge tank, with a lofty column in the centre.

One could hardly look without a shudder at the Secunder Bagh garden, one hundred and twenty yards square, where the English troops in 1857 took their revenge by slaughtering, to a man, two thousand sepoys. The drive through Wingfield Park, which contains many singular trees, *e.g.*, the bael and the fragrant sandal-wood, was exceedingly pleasant. It led us to the Church Mission compound, containing some old buildings, very picturesque. The Kaiser Bagh is an enormous structure, a mass of plaster and stucco, in the Cremorne style of modern grandeur. Next we visited the Chowk, a long narrow bazaar, crowded with natives who made way and shrunk from us, not, we were told, out of respect to the conquering race, but from religious dread of contact and pollution. The great Imambara, "the architectural gem of Lucknow," is a huge edifice in the fort of great solidity, with a grand hall sixty yards long, and now converted into a depôt for ordnance. The elephant stables, a short distance from the city, give one a good idea of the majesty and docility of these creatures, when tame and employed on state occasions. Here upwards of a hundred tame elephants are kept by the Government, well-housed and fed, and all

IMAMBARA, LUCKNOW.

well trained—a marvellous sight, especially as we saw them, when all out on parade in a wide field, each with his mamouts or keepers. The cost of each elephant would probably make a fat living for a hundred Hindu families. The depôts where captured elephants are kept are called *Khedda*. They are usually captured in Eastern Bengal by being driven into V-shaped traps or corrals; and by degrees are broken in and tamed so as to become the most majestic and docile of beasts of burden. On state occasions these elephants are clad in the costliest cloths, surmounted by gilded howdahs.

PAVILION OF TURKA, KAISER BAGH, LUCKNOW.

But, of course, the centre of interest in Lucknow is the Residency, where, in 1857, two thousand two hundred souls, consisting of nearly a thousand European residents, with their women and children and native servants, who came in for refuge, and five hundred English soldiers, under Sir Henry Lawrence, with the same number of native soldiers who remained faithful, kept a large army of sepoys at bay for six months.

The building is a large three-storied house, with two towers, and thick walls, standing on an elevation. Its grounds cover some acres, with scattered buildings, and a rampart. It is a ruin, a melancholy spectacle; and the inscriptions are most affecting, "Here Sir Henry Lawrence was wounded;" "Here Sir Henry Lawrence died." We went down to the huge cellars,

STATE ELEPHANTS, WITH HOWDAHS, ON PARADE.

where the women and children and the sick took refuge. Marks of shot and shell are on every hand, but Nature has mantled the spot with verdure. Near is the burial-ground, sweet with blooming roses, but full of touching monuments raised over the remains of those who died of disease or were shot during the siege. July was the most fatal month. On the fourth of that month, Lawrence, the beloved, the adored commander, fell. His tomb has this inscription, embodying his own dying words: "Here lies Henry Lawrence, who tried to do his duty. May the Lord have mercy on his soul!" Nearly three months passed after his death before Havelock came to the rescue.

Soon afterwards, this great general himself died of disease, brought on by the hardships of his march. His tomb is at the Alambagh, and over it a monument erected by his widow and children, with the inscription: "He showed how the profession of a Christian could be combined with the duties of a soldier." To his friend Outram, before he died, he said, "For more than forty years I have so ruled my life, that when death came, I might face it without fear."

RUINS OF THE RESIDENCY, LUCKNOW.

What with beautiful parks, capital roads, good shops, and a large civil and military population, Lucknow, in spite of these sad memories, is, we are told, extremely popular. There is plenty of society, and plenty of amusement. Boating, shooting, games of all sorts, are in vogue; Badminton parties, races, and "a magnificent ball-room with a perfect floor." Out of a native taxation amounting to twenty lakhs of rupees, the authorities of these North-West Provinces spend three and a half in "conservancy," including lighting, repairing, and watering the roads, and seven and a half on works of public utility; so that the European residents are well provided for. In the hottest months they have within easy reach by way of railway to Bareilly, the refreshing hill station of Naini Tal.

Naini Tal is in the Himâlayan division of Kumaon, and is the resort of the Government of the North-West Provinces during the hot weather. The scenery as we ride up is lovely; fine trees, drooping creepers, orchids, and tree ferns. The road winds round hills rising above hills, all densely wooded, with peeps into valleys, each divided by its stream. Unexpectedly, at last, a turn in the road reveals Naini Tal, a tarn rather than a lake, oval and olive green. "At the concave end of a horseshoe," says an accurate writer, "about the centre, place church, library, club, hotel, bazaar, and a few houses, almost encircling a beautiful lake elevated six thousand three hundred and fifty feet, the surrounding hills rising to eight thousand five hundred feet. Up the valley in the heart of the mountains cottages are scattered about, but the hotels and places of resort are located on the flat near the margin of the water. Lake circumference, two miles, depth ninety-three feet, with a ridge running through the centre twenty feet. People need never be dull. Quiet enough for those contented to walk round the Syren Lake, or to climb up the hills." The "snow seat" commands a magnificent view. The rhododendrons are large, with thick trunks and splendid blossoms. "I made," says Mr. Shiell, "a ten days' walking tour from Naini Tal towards 'the snows' through those hills, and woods, and waters that make Kumaon the fairest portion of all the sub-Himâlayan region, one of the most beautiful territories upon earth. Alone in all that great extent it possesses lake scenery, a chain of gem-like tarns stretching some fifteen to twenty miles from Naini Tal. As we progressed to Almorah, the snows grew nearer and more vast. The farthest point we reached was a hill called Binsur Peak, a tree-clad isolated cone; the warm tints of sunset suffused the snows with a hectic flush, which, gradually, as the sun declined, faded from off them, till they grew pale and cold, like marble masks, and the stars came out, one by one, flickering like tapers on the faces of the dead."

SCENE NEAR NAINI TAL.

An awful landslip took place at Naini Tal on the 18th of September, 1880.

About one o'clock in the day the place was startled by a sudden and sullen roar, louder than the crash of heavy guns, followed by a rumbling as of distant thunder, and then by an ominous silence. Vast clouds of dust rose heavenward, and the whole place shook as though an earthquake had passed. The waters of the lake rose in a moment far above their usual limit, and swept in a massive wave towards the weir. It was as though some giant had dropped half a mountain on the spot. Many lives were lost, several houses destroyed. Never was havoc more sudden, more awful, or more complete. Without a moment's warning

NAINI TAL GORGE, ALMORAH ROAD.

down came the enormous landslip, burying in deadly embrace the hotel and a party of workmen behind, assembly-rooms and library, with every living soul they contained. The station was plunged into the deepest gloom.

CAWNPORE, only forty miles by railway from Lucknow, is a busy, populous town, with cotton factories, flour mills, and large saddlery works. It is situated on the Ganges, which here varies in width from five hundred yards to a mile, and is crossed by a long railway bridge. The military station, with accommodation for seven thousand troops, is extremely

SUTTEE-CHAORA GHAT, GANGES, CAWNPORE.

popular with pig-stickers and sportsmen generally. It stands in a flat, sandy plain, very hot and dusty. Near the railway station, a fine old soldier of Havelock's army, who was in all the fighting of 1857, keeps an hotel, and acts as guide to his visitors. Our guide first led us over Wheeler's Entrenchment, now green and garden-like, where Sir Hugh Wheeler gathered two hundred and fifty men, the remnant of his troops, the rest having mutinied, three hundred residents and three hundred and thirty women and children. Here he defended himself bravely behind a slender rampart of earth for several weeks, when at length the worn-out band, already sadly reduced by death, yielded to the treacherous promises of the Nana Sahib and surrendered, with the issue that we all know. This is no place to tell again the heart-rending story. Enough that the WELL associated with these horrors is now surrounded by a monument touchingly appropriate and beautiful. It is by Marochetti, and walled in with a Gothic railing. The statue is that of an angel leaning with drooping wings, her back against the all-sustaining cross, her arms folded upon her breast, having in her hands the palm leaves emblematical of martyrdom and victory. The pedestal bears the following inscription :

"Sacred to the perpetual memory of a great company of Christian people—chiefly women and children—who, near this spot, were cruelly massacred by the followers of the rebel Nana Dhoondopunt of Bithoor, and cast, the dying with the dead, into the well below, on the fifteenth day of July, 1857."

A memorial church stands a short distance off, round which are many tombs. The inscription is frequent : "These are they which came out of great tribulation." One thinks of Cawnpore with a shudder, and leaves it with a sigh. The fact, however, must be recorded whenever the sad story is told, that the most careful Government investigations failed to discover a single case on the part of the sepoys of mutilation before death, or of torture, or of the dishonour of women during the Indian Mutiny.

MEMORIAL WELL, CAWNPORE.

"However late you arrive at AGRA, if it is moonlight, drive to the Taj." This was the advice of a friend who had seen the Taj, and who adored it as the finest sight on earth. "Be sure to have moonlight for Agra and the Taj," said another. Agra and the Taj seem to go together in the imagination of many, and Agra seems almost to exist for the Taj. "Nothing that has been written," says a third, "does the Taj any sort of justice, and we may wait another two hundred and fifty years for a worthy description." What then is the Taj? It is a tomb, a Mohammedan tomb, the tomb of a woman, the tomb of a rich man's favourite wife, the word Taj being, like "Sall," or "Bess," the pet name with which he addressed her ; it is her tomb and his own, for he lies beside her, built in compliance with a request of hers before she died. One characteristic of the Tartars was their tomb-building propensity. Each Mogul in turn built a tomb for himself. The Taj was built by the Mogul Shah Jehan, the grandson of Akbar, as a tomb for his favourite wife, Moomtaj a Mehal, and for himself. About two miles from the town along a dusty road, you pass under a colossal gateway, in itself an object commanding and impressive, and worth coming many miles to see; and before you is a lovely garden, green and shaded with beautiful trees, and in the centre an avenue of tall dark cypress-trees, separated by a line of fountains, and leading the eye to the foot of the building, which rises from a double platform, the first of red sandstone twenty feet high and one thousand feet broad, the second of marble fifteen feet high, and three hundred feet square, on the corners of which stand four marble minarets. In the centre

AGRA FORT.

of all thus reared in air stands the Taj, with giant arches and clustering domes. The afternoon sun was shining upon it, and the deep blue sky beyond. As you walk towards it the building grows to its real size, and what at first sight seemed a swan-like vision reared in air now displays its colossal proportions, a marble shrine of great magnitude inlaid with precious stones, graceful in its outlines, costly in its gems, and perfect in its details. Beyond, the Jumna flows; and on either side the great platform there rises a beautiful mosque, the one for use, the other (because not looking towards Mecca) raised only for finish and symmetry. Every picture of the Taj fails to give the full impression of its majesty, because with minuteness of detail, and effeminate elegance of finish it fails to embody its stupendous size and giant massiveness. What is huge and massive is usually associated in the mind with what is rough, abrupt, ponderous. In the Taj you have the majesty of a giant building combined with the lightness and delicacy of a costly cabinet. As Bishop Heber said, the Saracens built like Titans, and finished like jewellers. The Taj is, in fact, a colossal

THE TAJ MEHAL, AGRA.

casket, whose base is a square of one hundred and eighty-six feet, whose height is two hundred feet, and whose cost was above two millions sterling. The echoes under its dome are almost perpetual, and most soft and musical. Within, all is empty, save the marble sarcophagus above, and the actual tomb in a vault beneath. Death is there without any hopeful emblem, and to the triumph of death the building witnesses. As I walked round it outside the words came into my mind which the disciples addressed to Jesus: "Master, see what manner of stones and what buildings are here." Nor could I shut out from my recollection those other words of the Master in reply: "Seest thou these great buildings? There shall not be left one stone upon another that shall not be thrown down"—words which significantly stand in close connection with His estimate of the widow's mite, uttered a few moments before,—her act permanent, the massive temple transient. The Taj is a perfect casket, perfect in its proportions, its material, its elegance, its costliness; but it lacks object, sanctity, history, associations, utility. It is, as I have said, a tomb, the tomb of one of the wives of a Mohammedan ruler, built at her request for her and for himself. As a tomb, the grave of his faithful daughter, covered with sod, at Delhi, touches a higher chord. As a building, though with some it is a sign of culture to adore it as the embodiment of heavenly beauty, and comparable even with the eternal snows of the Himâlayas, to my mind, considering the national history and aspirations they each embody, the Parthenon at Athens, the cathedral at Milan, and even the Capitol at Washington, are nobler buildings than the Taj.

BALCONY IN PALACE, AGRA.

The palaces of the Moguls in India are usually found within the fort of the capital. The fort of Agra though hardly equal to that of Delhi, is grand and imposing. It is of red sandstone, and its walls are forty feet high. Within are the various buildings belonging to the palace of a Mohammedan ruler. There is a hall of public audience, and one of

PEARL MOSQUE, AGRA.

private audience, luxurious chambers and baths, dwellings for the soldiers, dungeons for prisoners, throne-rooms, and mosques for worship. Here are stored the Somnath Gates, the dumb memorials of Lord Ellenborough's pompous and silly boast. Here the great Akbar lived for many years. But the most beautiful buildings here were raised by his grandson, Shah Jehan. These consist of the apartments of the harem, and the Pearl Mosque. As to the harem, "picture to yourselves," says a graphic writer, "rooms or boudoirs, call them what you please, opening one into another, all of pure marble; here a balcony supported by delicate pillars with projecting roofs; there, exquisite balustrades in delicate lace-like open patterns, having no ornament, save gilding, with views extending over the country, and embracing the Taj and the Jumna. Imagine, again, rivulets of water streaming from room to room along marble beds; gardens of flowers and precious exotics; the creepers running over trellises, and shading from the heat the pathways across the marble floors, and mingling with the flying spray of the fountains; and this on and on from room to room, from balcony to balcony, from court to court."

Pre-eminent in beauty, within the fort of Agra is the Mutee Musjid, or Pearl Mosque, also built by Shah Jehan, two hundred and forty feet from east to west, and one hundred and ninety feet from north to south, with an open court one hundred and fifty feet square. This building is wholly of white marble, from the pavement to the summit of its domes. The western part or mosque proper is also of white marble, except an Arabic inscription from the Koran in black. The domes tower high above the other buildings of the fort, and in the glare of the morning sun look as if really built up of pearl. It is not only the Pearl Mosque, it is the pearl of mosques, unequalled in beauty by any other.

But to all this white marble there is a dark side, "dark scenes in the shades below balancing the brilliant scenes in the heights above. Deep down are seen mysterious stairs descending into empty cells and covered vaults, and from these again descending deeper and deeper still, through tortuous passages, ending apparently in nothing, yet with more than a suspicion of a something beyond, although a built-up wall interposes. We examined these mysterious and dim retreats, and we saw enough to convince us that pleasure and pain, 'lust and hate,' were near neighbours in Agra, as in other places. Sad evidences were apparent of beings who from jealousy, or other causes, had been conveyed to these chambers of horror, and there executed in the eye of God alone." Beyond some of these barriers human skeletons have been found, some hung with ropes. Thus, side by side with the relics of Oriental splendour, are the visible tokens of Mogul cruelty.

The tomb of Akbar is near Secundra, seven miles from Agra, in a court a quarter of a mile square. A heavy wall surrounds it like a fortress. It is three hundred feet square, and a hundred feet high, rising in terraces of pyramidal form, with cloisters, galleries, and domes. The design is borrowed, Mr. Fergusson thinks, from a Hindu, or, more correctly, a Buddhist model. The highest elevation is flat-roofed, with kiosks at the angles. Omit the domes, and the resemblance to the old Buddhist viharas is apparent. Akbar was just and tolerant, and sought in vain to abolish the distinction between Hindu and Mohammedan. He abolished the Hindu tax, jiziah, and carried out many reforms. He took up his residence at Futtepore Sikri, where are to be seen his finest works as a builder, which cluster, Acropolis-like, upon the top of a small ridge of hills. The richest of these are three pavilions, said to have been erected for his three favourite sultanas. But his most majestic work is the mosque, sternly grand ; the southern gateway of which stands on a rising ground, and "when looked at from below is noble," says Mr. Fergusson, "beyond that of

GATEWAY AT SECUNDRA.

any portal attached to any mosque in India, perhaps in the whole world." Futtepore Sikri was the Windsor or Versailles of the Moguls. It is twenty miles from Agra, on a rocky hill ; and the wall enclosing it is nine miles in extent. Among the buildings, one is called the Hide-and-Seek Palace, with narrow corridors, where, as is told, the consorts of the emperor used to amuse themselves at bo-peep. The material of the buildings is red sandstone, of the richest colour and finest grain. "The style," acutely observes Mr. Sheill, "though elaborately ornate, is characterised by an almost grim severity ;

and so cyclopean are the dimensions and the massiveness of the masonry that they might be the abodes of an extinct race of giants."

The seat of government in the North-West Provinces is ALLAHABAD, "City of Allah," a Mohammedan name, given in the sixteenth century to the ancient Prayâga, a sacred Hindu city situated on the tongue of land formed by the confluence of the Jumna and the Ganges. A magnificent railway bridge now spans the Jumna just above the union of the rivers. Its length is three thousand two hundred and twenty-four feet, and there are fifteen openings of two hundred and five feet clear. The piers are of stone,

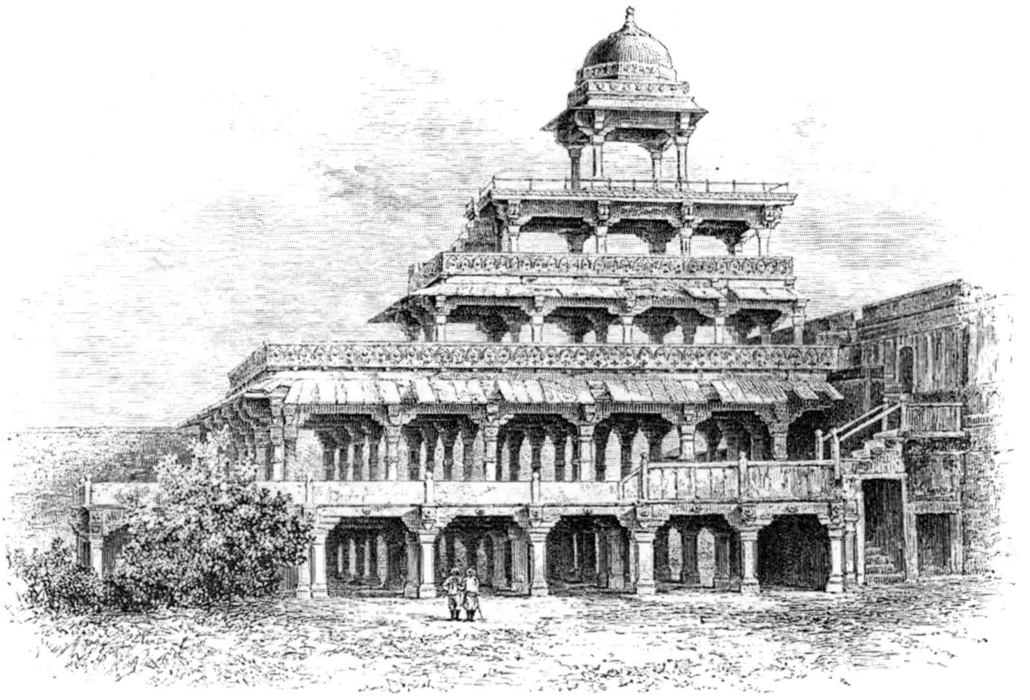

PANCH MAHAL, FUTTEPORE SIKRI.

sunk fifty feet below the bed of the river. It reminds one somewhat of the bridge at Montreal. Allahabad was once a republican state in the heart of ancient India. The fort, originally a Hindu stronghold, but rebuilt by Akbar of red stone, though not to be compared with that of Agra, contains a monolith forty-two feet high, with a Pali inscription—one of those erected by the Buddhist King Asoka. This is the most complete and probably the oldest of the Buddhist Lâts. Under the great hall, now transformed into an arsenal, steps lead down to a subterranean Hindu temple, full of loathsome figures and emblems daubed with red paint. No doubt the place was originally a Buddhist cave-temple. The stump of a banyan tree, said to be fifteen centuries old, and still alive, is here the object of worship. A light burns before it, and beside it a young Brahman sits to receive the offerings of the devotees. As we stood near, some women came up, paid their money, received the priest's blessing, scattered flowers, and then embraced with kisses the sacred stump. At Delhi and Agra Hinduism has been crushed by Mohammedanism. At Allahabad it has taken refuge underground. From the roof of the arsenal we looked upon the junction of the Jumna and the Ganges, where many pilgrims were bathing. This "meeting of the waters" is regarded as a most sacred place of pilgrimage, and in January and February during the *Mêla* it presents the appearance of a continual fair, with processions, banners, booths, and bathers. Thousands go down into the water, all classes and all ages, in the vain hope of washing away their guilt.

The Sarai in Allahabad is a square high-walled garden, containing three stone Mohammedan mausoleums, surmounted by marble domes. They are the tombs of the two sons of Jehanjir and their mother. That in the centre, of the unhappy Khusru, the eldest son, and victim of his father's cruelty, is the largest;

BRIDGE OVER THE GANGES, OUDE AND ROHILKANT RAILWAY.

that of the mother, on the right, comes next; but they do not allow her to have a quiet sleep, for the upper floor of her tomb has been fitted up into a billiard-room. That of the younger son, on the left, is smaller, and is surmounted by a graceful dome. The walls of all three are outwardly ornamented, and the interiors are beautifully painted, though the colours are faded. Near the Sarai is the pretty church of the Episcopal Methodist Mission, which is very successful among the Hindus. The American Presbyterian Mission, whose operations stretch far up into the Punjab, has its head-quarters here, and its schools are most efficient. It has asylums for the blind and for lepers, a printing-press and depository. Allahabad, as the great railway centre where the lines from Delhi, Calcutta and Bombay meet, is a rapidly-growing city.

TOMBS IN THE SARAI, ALLAHABAD.

TEMPLE OF AMRITSAR AND LAKE OF IMMORTALITY.

THE PUNJAB.

BAS-RELIEFS IN THE MUSEUM, PESHÂWAR.

THE PUNJAB.

ITS CONDITION AND EXTENT—DELHI AND ITS PLAINS—AMRITSAR AND LAHORE—PESHÂWAR AND KASHMIR—SIMLA—LANDOUR—DHARMSALA—DALHOUSIE.

WATER-CARRIERS.

THE Punjab is the most promising of English conquests in India. It is nearest to England by way of Karâchi; it has a cooler and more bracing climate, though the south parts about Multan are almost rainless, and from the proximity of the desert the air becomes scorching. It has accessible hill stations, and it has a population of twenty-three millions, friendly and loyal, as well as quiet and industrious. "When I first crossed the Sutlej," says the lamented John Lawrence, "there was not the trace of a road in the country, now we have several thousand miles of road and railways. The people were our enemies; one class in the country preyed on the other; there was little real security. Now all this has changed. Life and property are wonderfully safe. The people are peaceable and well-disposed.

All this has been proved beyond question in 1857, when, but for the general contentment of the people, it would not have been possible to maintain the public tranquillity, still less to have assisted in the re-conquest of Hindustan. For all these advantages I acknowledge myself indebted to the great Author of all good. Without His guiding and protecting hand, what would indeed have become of us all?" Henry and John Lawrence, and indeed most of their coadjutors and successors in the government of the Punjab, were men who openly avowed their faith in Christianity, and their desire to give it to the people they governed. They supported missionary effort, and the results are evident. Sir Herbert Edwardes, the Commissioner, openly declared at Peshâwar: "The East has been given to our country for a mission, neither to the minds nor bodies, but to the souls of men. Our mission in India is to do for other nations what we have done for our own. To the Hindus we have to preach one God, and to the Mohammedans to preach one Mediator." The Americans were the pioneers of missions throughout the district; and the foundations of a sound Bible Christianity have been deeply laid. Besides efficient schools, they have founded orphanages, asylums, and hospitals. No fewer than eight Missionary Societies, with thirty central missions, are now at work in the Punjab; and no stronger argument for Christian missions could be urged than that afforded by the state of the country.

The name Punjab signifies "the five rivers," the five great tributaries of the Indus; and the tracts of country between the rivers are called Doabs. But the Sutlej, the limit of the conquests of Alexander the Great, does not form the eastern boundary. The province of Delhi itself has since the Mutiny been included; and when one enters Delhi one enters the Punjab. Many hill states are also embraced under the name; and to these must be added ill-governed Kashmir, extending beyond the Himâlayas, and unjustly handed over to the tender mercies of an alien Maharajah.

DELHI, the Rome of Asia during three thousand years, is a thousand miles from Calcutta, and fifteen hours by railway from Cawnpore. The city is on the river Jumna, just outside the boundary of the North-West Provinces, and within the Punjab. It had a long history before the Moguls. It is said to have been destroyed and rebuilt seven times; and the remains of these successive cities cover the plain for miles. The great fort, built by Shah Jehan, is a mile and a half in circuit, with a wall forty feet high. Entering by the Lahore Gate, a splendid Gothic arch in the centre of the tower is succeeded by a long vaulted aisle; and driving through, we come to the Hall of Public Audience, of red sandstone, and then by the Motee Musjid, the Mosque of Pearls, well named from its pearly loveliness, to the Hall of Private Audience, all of polished marble, and looking out over the wide Jumna. Here, between each pair of pillars, is a beautiful balustrade of marble chastely carved. The roof has at each corner a marble kiosk with a gilt dome. The ceiling is composed of gold and silver filigree work, and in the centre stood the famous peacock throne of solid gold, with gems and diamonds estimated as worth six million pounds sterling. It was

HALL OF PRIVATE AUDIENCE, DELHI.

captured by the Persian Nadir Shah in 1739. All this wealth and grandeur have been taken away; but the building still witnesses to its former magnificence, and along the cornice on each side of the chamber the inscription is repeated in flourishing Arabic inlaid: "If there be a paradise on earth, it is this! it is this! it is this!" *Vanitas vanitatum*, would be a more appropriate motto now.

The great Mosque of Delhi, built of red sandstone and white marble—the snowy domes marble, the needle-like minarets red sandstone — perched high upon a rock, and approached by forty deep steps on three of its sides, is the one object that meets the eye everywhere about Delhi, and is the finest mosque in India, and the chief shrine of Indian Mohammedanism. Like all great mosques, it is named Jumma Musjid, *i.e.* the Friday Mosque, Friday being the Mohammedan Sabbath. The Empress, our Queen, has forty millions of Mohammedan subjects in India. Their bearing strikes you

JUMMA MUSJID, DELHI.

at once as different from that of the Hindus. They are conquered conquerors. Once the rulers, they are in turn the ruled; and as they walk haughtily along, when they pass an Englishman, they grind their teeth. Pride and hatred, the two most prominent features in a Mohammedan, are apparent on every hand. To describe this mosque will be to describe all. A huge quadrangle open to the sky, four hundred and fifty feet square, a fountain in the middle, for the ablutions of the faithful, a colonnade on three sides, north, south and east, of red sandstone with open arches. On the west, towards Mecca, a building open in front, of white marble, covered with three graceful white marble domes, surmounted by spires of copper, richly gilt. Its front—with a majestic opening in the centre and smaller arches on either side—is all of white marble with Arabic inscriptions. The interior is paved throughout with nine hundred immense oblong slabs of white marble bordered with black, and in the wall, at the centre, is the niche, or *kibla,* towards sacred Mecca, where prayers are directed. At either corner is a minaret one hundred and forty feet high, of white marble and red sandstone placed vertically in alternate stripes. Up these the muezzin goes to call to prayers; and the summit commands a magnificent view. On Fridays you may see the vast area filled with worshippers kneeling

CLOISTERS, MOSQUE OF KUTUB, NEAR DELHI.

and rising, standing up and prostrating themselves as one man. Women are seldom seen within the precincts; indeed, practically, women, according to the Mohammedans, have no souls, they exist for and are the chattels of men. The Koran itself allows a man four wives, to say nothing of concubines; and its paradise is a paradise of lust. It is the fashion to praise Mohammed and the Koran; but history, and the present character of the Moslems of every land, testify that whatever excellence there may appear in the founder or his great work, hatred, cruelty, pride and lust are the graces which it fosters. From treating his women with savage coolness, or beating them with rage, the Mohammedan will turn towards Mecca, and in pharisaic devoutness taking off his shoes and spreading his garment in the most conspicuous place, he will go through his gesticulations and perform his prayers. Here in Delhi, at Agra, Allahabad, and Bombay, in Cairo, Jerusalem, Damascus, Constantinople, London, by land and on board ship, I have witnessed the performance, and always has it left this impression on my mind.

There are in the neighbourhood of what we may call the Mohammedan Delhi the ruins of a series of successive cities that have been razed to the ground. Among these stands the Lât of Feroz Shah, a monolith of red sandstone covered with an inscription in Pali, which tells that it was erected by Asoka. The column is, therefore, at least two thousand two hundred years old, and the inscription upon it is probably the oldest writing in India. The tomb of Humayun, Akbar's father, a tyrant of great cruelty, the patron of Thuggism, and now revered as a saint, is colossal in size and marvellous in workmanship; red sandstone inlaid with marble, and white marble domes. It took sixteen years in building, and the quadrangle of solid masonry in which it stands is four hundred yards square. Near it is the sixty-four pillared hall, and a beautifully-carved tomb of a Mussulman saint of the fourteenth century. Another sumptuous tomb is in honour of a scoundrel who killed himself by drinking cherry-brandy, of which liquor he used to swallow a glass an hour! Here also is the simple sodded grave of the faithful daughter of Shah Jehan, faithful to him when he was imprisoned by his son in the midst of his grandeur, and with the inscription on a stone at the head in Arabic: "Let no rich canopy cover my grave. This grass is the best covering for the tomb of the poor in spirit." Such simplicity is refreshing amid gigantic idolatry in stone of man and the basest of men. At hand, in a small deep tank, forty feet square, miserable Hindus turn a penny by jumping with a run from a dome top, feet foremost from a height of fifty feet, shooting like arrows straight into the water, with the sound of a dead man's dive, and presently coming up to you quite exhausted to beg backsheesh for the feat.

After traversing the wide sandy plain covered with these buildings and ruins for a distance of eleven miles, it is a relief to reach an oasis of green sward and shady trees. Here, in the midst of verdure, stand the most gigantic and impressive remains of old Delhi's splendour. Passing through Aladin's Gate, a majestic arch, reminding one almost of Furness Abbey, and with the celebrated iron pillar about fifty feet in length before it, you see before you a massive column like an isolated minaret with five successive galleries. This is the celebrated KUTUB MINAR, a fluted column two hundred and forty feet high, one hundred feet circumference at the base, and gradually diminishing in a series of five stories, like joints in a telescope, to thirty feet circumference at the summit. The view from the top is extensive, modern Delhi and the hills beyond being perfectly clear in outline. What the column was built for it is difficult to say. It is supposed to be, not a Mohammedan, but a Hindu building, dating from the twelfth century; but it certainly looks much more like the Moslem buildings in modern Delhi; and the more probable tradition is that it was erected in 1193 to celebrate the overthrow of the last of

ALADIN'S GATE, WITH IRON PILLAR.

the Hindu Rajahs of Delhi. A sultan named *Katub*, who succeeded Ghori (A.D. 1206), a general and administrator, is said to have built this *minar* or "pillar" of victory. Round about it are the ruins of a mosque, built out of the previous ruins of Hindu temples, like the cloisters of a great cathedral. The enigmatical iron pillar, sixty feet long, smooth and black with age, and the elaborately-carved columns of the temple indicate a Brahmanical origin. In the midst of these ruins the trees and shrubs and creepers are most luxuriant and refreshing after the heat and dust and glare of the plain.

The Siege of Delhi was one of the most tragic and important events of the Mutiny year. In the Chowk, or main thoroughfare, seventy-four feet wide, with a raised shaded footpath running down the centre and planted with trees, Captain Hodson exposed the bodies of the aged King of Delhi's two sons, whom he had himself shot without trial and with his own hand after their surrender. In this street, too, stands the kotwali, or court-house, before which the defenders of the city during the siege were one after another executed by the English. The inhabitants may well tremble at the very name of this street. But it is very gay; full of shops, in fact, it is called the Regent Street of Delhi, which now glories in Lord Lytton's burlesque Durbar of 1876, held while famine was stalking through the peninsula, and preparing its holocaust of five million souls. Delhi

KUTUB MINAR, NEAR DELHI.

is a convenient, sociable, and popular station for the judicial, military, and revenue officers. Driving to the Ridge outside the city to the north, we passed through the Kashmir Gate, blown up bravely by the English when they stormed the city; and close by it is the spot where Nicholson fell, who, as his tombstone tells, led the assault of Delhi, but was in the hour

CHANDI CHOWK, DELHI.

of victory mortally wounded. Crowning the height, a mile away, and commanding a magnificent view over Delhi, is the Flagstaff Tower; and, farther on, the Memorial, appropriately giving on its sides the details of encampment and of siege. It bears the inscription: "In memory of the officers and soldiers of the Delhi field force who were killed in action or died of wounds or disease between the 30th of May and the 20th of September, 1857. Erected by their comrades and government."

Turning from these sad reminiscences it was a relief on the Sunday to attend Christian services and to mark the progress of Christian missions. The name of England is in North India associated everywhere so palpably with troops, cantonments, battles and bloodshed, that were it not for missions and missionaries there would be nothing to show that our country is also associated with the Gospel of the Prince of Peace. It is an old native proverb, "English religion, devil religion." Bayonets rather than Bibles, gunpowder rather than goodness, are associated with our country in native experience. Even attendance at church is accompanied with the clank of swords and the beat of drums. Still the Christian religion is not without its champions and its votaries in the army as well as outside. Missionaries are often the objects of careless hilarious ridicule at other tables besides mess tables, but usually on the part of men who do not really know them nor take any pains to examine their work. For the most part their lives are quiet and obscure; but they are nevertheless the true and consistent ambassadors of the Prince of Peace and King of Righteousness. Here in Delhi the Cambridge mission is making its way among different classes of the inhabitants. There is a square of houses on the north-east of the city occupied almost entirely by native Christians; and several weekly Bible classes are attended by Hindus. The high schools have many Christian native teachers. The Baptists have been in Delhi sixty years, and have an extensive field of operations. Their ragged schools receive, like most mission schools in India, Government aid, and are doing a very good work among the poorest classes, teaching the pupils to read the Gospels. Their *Basti* meetings in the open air amid the dwellings of the poor after the day's work is done are attended by from fifty to a hundred heathens or Mohammedans. There are five-and-twenty places where these singing meetings are held three or four evenings a week. The tunes are native. The Zenana Mission is also effectively worked, and many women are under Christian influence and instruction.

Leaving Delhi at 1.30 P.M. and travelling all night north-west by railway three hundred and sixteen miles, we find ourselves next morning at six o'clock in Amritsar, "fountain of immortality," a great emporium of trade, and the sacred city of the religious community called Sikhs. The word *Sikhs* signifies "disciples," and the religion thus designated is a mixture of Hinduism and Mohammedanism, inculcating the worship of one God, but attaching extreme reverence to the cow. The spiritual teachers of these "disciples" are called Gurus; and many of the population, including most of the upper classes, are of this persuasion. Its Bible is called the *Grunth*, and is regarded with great reverence. It has been translated into English, and the translator describes it as "shallow and incoherent in the extreme."

Amritsar is a very oriental-looking city, and a great place for ivory carving and for the manufacture of Kashmir shawls. The process is exceedingly tedious and trying to the workman's eyes. A separate shuttle is used for every colour, and a whole day may be spent over a section of the shawl scarcely perceptible to the eye. The rooms in which they are woven are close and narrow, in fact, dirty and wretched dens, a strange contrast

GOLDEN TEMPLE OF THE SIKHS, AMRITSAR.

to the picturesque city outside. But the one great sight of Amritsar is the Golden Temple of the Sikhs. It is of pure white marble, rising out of a large tank, and its roof is of plates of copper richly gilded. The blue rippling waves wash against the polished marble courtyard which surrounds the tank. The temple is connected by a broad roadway, also of white marble, with golden balustrades and lamps (see frontispiece to this volume). The lower half of the walls are carved white marble, the doors solid silver, the windows golden; while the upper half and the roof seem a mass of gold. The outside dazzles, glistening in the brilliant sunlight, and is reflected in the sparkling waters. There is much mosaic work in the marble flooring, and the interior is highly gilded. The temple is not large, but somewhat resembles the Alhambra.

Lahore is only two hours by railway from Amritsar. It was a great city a thousand years ago. In the time of the Moguls it is said to have

TOMB OF RUNGIT SING, LAHORE.

had a circumference of eighteen miles. But now it is a mere shadow of its former self. It is only about three miles in circumference, and a circular road runs round it with a belt of ornamental garden. The Great Mosque built by Aurangzeb is a stately pile, and has in its quadrangle a noble banyan and other trees peopled with flocks of starlings. But, like that at Benares, the mosque is deserted. The high perched white fort commands an admirable view of the city and the dusty wilderness around. One of the chief sights in Lahore is the tomb erected by the beautiful and talented Nurjehan over her drunken husband, the Emperor Jehanjeer. It is in the style of the Taj, and stands in a beautiful garden planted with orange groves far to the west of the city across the Ravee.

The European quarters, including the military station, cover an area of fourteen square miles. The distances are quite awful. In the Lawrence Hall Gardens are eighty thousand trees. The residence of the Lieutenant-governor is opposite. Three miles from Mianmir, the military station, where

SAKHI SARWAR.

there is a splendid church, are the stately Shalamar Gardens. The church in the civil station is said to have been originally the tomb of a dancing-girl.

Two hundred miles south-west by rail, over arid desert from Lahore, lies MULTAN, well known for its dust storms and fiery heat, but of historic interest from Alexander the Great downwards, till it was taken by the British in 1849. It contains many mosques and a beautiful Hindu temple. Westward across the Indus is Dera Ghazi Khan; and thirty miles beyond, at the foot of the Suliman range, running north and south as a natural wall separating Afghanistan, is SAKHI SARWAR, said to be the place of which it was remarked by some native that, it being in existence, it was unnecessary for the gods to have made Hell also, the

STREET IN PESHÂWAR.

heat, dust and barrenness are choking and oppressive. The name is derived from that of a Mohammedan saint whose tomb close by, a large square tower-like building with spires or minarets, draws many pilgrims.

An annual festival or fair in his honour is held in the month of April. The walls of the shrine within are hung with small pillows variously ornamented, offerings of the pilgrims to the saint. Near the building is a defile called the Robber's Leap, enclosed with cliffs formed of gravelly layers, and rocks uneasily resting in fantastic positions. Farther on is a cave with the finger-print of the saint, and again the print of his left foot on a slanting ledge of rock; this place is called the *Moza*. His companions are said to be buried in an adjacent mound, on which are only pebbles and stunted brambles.

ATTOCK.

The Northern State Railway now runs all the way to Peshâwar, crosses the Jhelum (the ancient Hystaspes) near the Manikyala Tope, and passes through Rawal Pindee, a healthy military station situated on an elevated ridge. From this station we ascend in ten or twelve hours' dhooly journey to Murree, a gay and festive hill station upon a ridge seven thousand five hundred feet high. Northwards the slopes are clothed with oaks, pines and horse-chestnuts. Srinagur, the capital of Kashmir, is one hundred and sixty miles from Murree. Sixty miles beyond Rawal Pindee the railway brings us to Attock, a fortress on the Indus, which here is two hundred and sixty yards wide and flows in a strong turbulent torrent, crossed only by a bridge of boats. Overhanging the river is a crag looking out upon a wide tract of desert. Near to this Darius crossed the Indus, B.C. 518; and not far from Rawal Pindee Alexander the Great won his famous victory over Porus, B.C. 326. Forty miles more bring us to PESHÂWAR, the frontier-city, eighteen miles east of the Kyber Pass. Peshâwar has fifty thousand inhabitants, but its liability to earthquakes gives the buildings an unstable character. In the museum there are several interesting bas-reliefs, illustrative of early Indian sculpture, and showing the influence of Greek art. What the Buddhists were to the architecture of Northern India the Greeks were to its sculpture. Greek faces constantly occur in ancient Buddhist statuary, and the blending of these with Hindu forms and features is distinctly traceable. As by degrees Greek influence faded away, the coarser representations of full-blown Hinduism asserted their sway, as at Amravati and Sanchi, and afterwards at Elephanta.

BAS-RELIEFS IN THE MUSEUM, PESHÂWAR.

From Peshâwar may be seen the dark range of serrated mountains with the black chasm of the Kyber Pass, and far away the Hindu Koosh. The beautiful valley in the flush of spring when the horseshoe of mountains is still clad in snow, while its peach and quince gardens are in full flower, must be enchanting. The climate is temperate.

Another way into Kashmir is by the pretty station of Sealkote, which Mr. Grant Duff describes as the prettiest in India, the Pir Punjal and other great Himâlayan ranges being full in view. He was journeying to Jummoo, the winter capital of the Maharajah of Kashmir. "We had crossed most of the woodland, and had descended from our elephants, when we reached a point where in the clearer morning, the mountains stood out in all their beauty. On the left stretched the mighty snowy chain of the Pir Punjal, rising eighteen thousand feet. Then in the middle of the background came an outer range not snowy; lastly, far to the right another snowy range on the borders of Thibet. Between us and the mountains lay Jummoo, with its white pyramidal temples shining in the sun, and surrounded by a near landscape which wanted nothing to make it perfect. It was the most beautiful land view I ever beheld. The Maharajah is a lucky man, with heaven for his winter, and the seventh heaven for his summer capital."

BAS-RELIEFS IN THE MUSEUM, PESHÂWAR.

The easiest way, however, into "the Happy Valley," is by way of Rawal Pindee and Murree; and Mr. Anthony Shiell has given us a graphic account of the journey. The distance is a hundred and sixty miles, occupying five days on pony, and two by boat (doongah) on the river. The vale of Kashmir is an oval, a hundred miles long and twenty-five broad, traversed by the Jhelum and fringed by glens and minor valleys, encompassed by the snow-wall of the Himâlaya. Midway is the capital, Srinagur, with a population of 150,000. It lies upon a flat, intersected by canals; diversified by orchards, and lined by stately poplars. It is, like Venice, a city of canals, and a city of bridges—"Kandals" as they are called—quaint structures, centuries old, of "the incorruptible Himâlayan cedar, the invaluable deodara." There are two lakes, one celebrated for its historic and poetic associations, the other for the snowy mountains which it reflects. The river Jhelum forms the main thoroughfare of the city. Buildings cluster on either side down to the water's edge, mostly high four-storied wooden houses with pent roofs, overlaid with earth which is clothed with grass and other plants, and broad flights of stone steps lead down to the stream. The narrow streets are little better than the beds of open sewers. The panorama of mountains from the splintered crests of Pir Panjal on the south, to the broad brow of hoary Haramook on the north, and the snowy summit of "the Naked Mountain," is magnificent. The hill called "The Throne of Solomon," six thousand two hundred and sixty-three feet above the sea, and a thousand feet above the valley, has a

FLOATING GARDENS, LAKE OF SRINAGUR.

stone Buddhist temple on the top, now converted into a mosque. The panoramic view from this point is very grand of Peri Mahal Fort, Apple-tree Canal, and Poplar Avenue, and of the city lake, with the gardens, summerhouses and fountains, where lay the scene of *Lalla Rookh.* To the west lies Gulmarg, a favourite sanitarium, on a mountain common high up the hills, three thousand feet above Srinagur, the air cold, bracing and salubrious, and the plateau surrounded by forests of pine. Forty miles to the east and up the Himâlayas is the cave of Ambernath, a place of pilgrimage sacred to Siva, who is said "to have had the coolness to assume" the form of a block of ice and to take up his abode here. The cave is visited by thousands of pilgrims in July. It lies far up the Laddar Valley, sixteen thousand feet above the sea. It is of gypsum, fifty yards deep and fifty wide, thirty yards high. The scenery is of titanic splendour, and there is a noble glacier, with red-sandstone serrated cliffs rising one thousand feet on either side the defile.

From the railway at Umballa you drive northwards thirty-eight miles in Tonga Dâk,—a covered spring-cart drawn by a pair of ponies, with a centre board which divides the two front from the two back passengers—to

SHOPS, SRINAGUR, KASHMIR.

Kalka, from which place there are two roads, the old road and the new road, to SIMLA. The old road is a difficult mountain path, up which if you are not carried in a sort of sedan, called "a jampan," you had better ride or walk. The views are commanding all the way. The new road is a masterpiece of engineering, cut out of the sides of the mountains, and supported in many places by massive walls. The gradients are nicely adjusted, and you can drive the fifty-seven miles in eight hours by Tonga Dâk. Simla is seven thousand feet above the sea, and fir-clad Jacko eight thousand. What with graceful deodaras, firs, oaks, rhododendrons, the magnificent scenery and the snow panorama, Simla is exceedingly beautiful. The rain and mist in June and July are dismal in the extreme; but from October the weather is enchanting. Simla is the seat of the Supreme Government for half the year, "where it slumbers with a revolver under its pillow;"

and it is therefore a place full of caste and cost, a sort of Indian Olympus, from whose heights the officials living at Government expense look down with disdain upon the toilers in the plains beneath. It may be called a third heaven of flirtation and fashion. Indeed, one part is called Elysium. It is, as we say, "out of the world;" but it seems when you get there as if the world with its pomps and vanities had been caught up hither out of the world. It is an Indian Capua. You look over a billowy sea of hills to

SIMLA.

the great snowy range fifty miles away, its icy pinnacles glistening in the silent air as far as the eye can reach. The bazaar slopes gradually down the valley. The snows as seen from Simla are not so striking; but from neighbouring mountains, such as the Chore summit, the sacred sources of the Ganges can be seen, as represented by domes, towers and pinnacles of dazzling snow. It is a glorious tour, occupying about a month to go from Simla by Kotgur, where the Church Mission has a station, over the Burunghatti, fifteen thousand feet above the sea level.

LANDOUR, which is the oldest of the hill stations, lies about a hundred miles east of Simla, and is usually approached by way of Saharunpore, from which railway-station an omnibus runs along a well-metalled, shaded, undulating road, across the Sewalic range and dipping into a lovely valley, the Deyra Doon, to Rajpore. From Rajpore the remaining nine miles may be accomplished on foot by pony or in jampan. The road passes over deep precipices, and troops of monkeys, and here and there peacocks, may be seen as we climb. Passing through Mussoorie—sometimes called the Ramsgate of India—we reach Landour, on the crest of the mountain. There is not an acre of level land in view. It is a simple line of peaks, but every rock on which a house could be fastened has been seized upon, until villages of considerable size have sprung up. Roads, houses, and gardens have ingeniously been cut or scooped out of the hill-sides. Some white cottages cling like limpets to the ledges. The magnificent views have been thus described: "On one side lies the Deyra Doon, one of the fairest valleys in all the East, smiling in its verdure and foliage, although it was now mid-winter. Farther on is the Sewalic range of the Himalayas, and still farther, in full view, the great plain of India, fifteen hundred miles in extent, with the silvery threads of the Jumna and Ganges. On the opposite side, towards the north-east, separated by a confused mass of mountain, much of which is densely wooded, peak after peak of the snowy range, stretching out into Thibet and Kashmir, lifts its snowy head into the clouds." We are in the presence of the highest mountains on the globe, on the border of that table-land which the Arabs call "the roof of the world." Wilson, the author of *The Abode of Snow*, says, "There is nothing in the Alps which can afford even a faint idea of the savage desolation and appalling sublimity of many of the Himâlayan scenes. Nowhere have the faces of the rocks been so scarred and riven by the nightly action of frost, and the mid-day floods from melting snow. In almost every valley we see places where whole peaks or sides of great mountains have very recently come shattering down." The climate of Landour is delightful; "its warmth," says the eastern proverb, "is not heat, its coolness is not cold." Perhaps the purest air breathed by man is found in the Himâlayas, close to the snows, and at Landour it is almost as good, except where tainted by man. It is said to be the very best place in India for European children.

The hill stations for the Punjab are Dharmsala and Dalhousie. DHARMSALA is noted for excessive rains. In other parts of the Himâlayas the effect of the snow mountains is softened by intermediate ranges, but here they seem almost to overhang the spectator. Looking up from Kangra, the lower hills are like ripples on the sea, and the eye rests on the sublime titanic rocks sharp cut against the sky. The winding streams, the irrigated valley, said to be next to Cashmir in beauty, the bamboo clumps, the branching oaks, the stately pines, the blooming rhododendra, the ruins of hill castles, the towering old

PINDREE GLACIER, HIMÂLAYAS.

Kangra Fort, combine to make this one of the most fascinating hill stations in India. Nothing can be more impressive than the hills and mountains here lit up in solitary splendour and savage beauty by the crimson glory of an autumn sunset. The cold grey rocks become rose pink, and as this fades the silvery moon sheds her sheen over the valley and the fir-clad hills, realising the sad solemnity of the most impressive funeral. Here Lord Elgin sickened and died in 1863.

DALHOUSIE is still farther to the north-west, and is by some reckoned as the best of the hill stations, but to reach it involves a long and fatiguing journey from Amritsar. It spreads over three hills, the highest of which is nearly eight thousand feet above the sea. Beyond is a charming and well-wooded forest, while the famous Needle Rock, the highest of the peaks here visible, rises to the height of twenty-one thousand feet.

TOPE OF SANCHI, NORTHERN GATE.

RAJPUTANA AND CENTRAL INDIA AGENCY.

PALACE OF BIRSING DEO, AND LAKE DATTIA.

RAJPUTANA AND CENTRAL INDIA AGENCY.

MOUNT ABU — UDAIPUR AND CHITTORE — AJMERE — JAIPUR — ALWÁR — GWALIOR — SONAGHUR — SANCHI — BHOPAL.

THE large district of Rajputana, made up of eighteen different native states, with a population of eleven millions, is traversed from north-east to south-west by a system of mountains called the Aravalis, west of which is desert, and east lie a number of interesting cities. A railway now runs from Delhi along the mountain ranges, and joins the Baroda line from the south. The Agent of the British Government lives at MOUNT ABU, which rises five thousand feet above the sandy plain, and encloses a lovely valley, and a small lake called the Pearl Lake. This is a majestic hill sacred both for Hindus and for Jains; and they have here four temples arranged in the form of a cross, built of white marble brought from a distance, and dating as far back as the eleventh century. That built by the Prince Vincala Sah, though plain outside, is magnificent within, but bearing marks of decay. It contains a colossal statue of the deified coryphæus of the Jains Parswanatha.

Eastward from Mount Abu is UDAIPUR, situated on a low ridge with two lakes, or rather summer tanks, for they are artificial, one of which faces the city and reflects its palaces. There are a few islands, on which are built handsome residences. Looking from the east, the view is striking; the placid waters reflect the buildings; and the palace, built of granite, a hundred feet high, overlooks the lake and the city. It is considered one of the finest buildings in Rajputana, and is sometimes compared to Windsor.

Eastward again from Udaipur is the ancient capital, CHITTORE, whose fortress is conspicuous from afar, perched upon a lofty rock, which stretches northwards about two miles, forming a plateau, still covered with the remains of departed splendour. Chittore was long the stronghold of Hindu independence against the wave of Mohammedan conquest. Its prince was called the Rana. Three times it was besieged and sacked. First in A.D. 1300, when Ala-ud-din volunteered to raise the siege, provided the Rana's wife, the beautiful Pudmani, were surrendered to him. She stipulated to enter the conqueror's camp attended by the ladies of her household. On the appointed day seven hundred litters accompanied her, each litter carried by six armed soldiers disguised as porters, and containing not ladies, but warriors armed to the teeth. A bloody fray ensued, but the plot failed, the husband and wife escaped, and the siege was renewed; and rather than surrender, thousands of the wives and daughters of the inhabitants performed the *johur*, *i.e.* immolated themselves upon burning piles of timber, while the men rushed out of the city and perished sword in hand. The second siege was under the Sultan of Guzerat in 1533, when the women performed another *johur*, the princess before dying sending her bracelet as a challenge to Humayun to be her avenger; and he afterwards fulfilled the pledge and restored the Rana. The third and final siege was in 1567, by the famous Akbar. The women again threw themselves on burning piles, while the men put on saffron garments and perished sword in hand. Chittore was thenceforward deserted, and the Rana sought refuge in the Aravali Hills, and founded Udaipur.

Within the ruined fortress are several antique buildings. Besides the palace of the Rana, which was a plain building, are two vast temples with tanks or reservoirs. Inscriptions upon them state that they were built out of the ruins of former temples, brought from Nagara, five miles north. The most striking of the two is the Temple of Vriji. The style of architecture is good, and the masonry excellent. Perhaps the most singular building among the ruins is the Pillar of Victory, erected in 1439, by the Rana. It stands on a platform fourteen yards square, and is a hundred and fifty feet high. There are nine stories, and on the summit is a lantern tower and a dome. The whole is one mass of elaborate sculpture in white marble, representing various subjects in Hindu mythology. The tower commands a glorious view of the country round.

A railway is being constructed which runs northwards from Indore through Chittore to Ajmere, and joins the Rajputana line. AJMERE is a city of great antiquity and interest, surrounded by a wall with five strong gateways in a beautiful style of architecture. It is in a lovely valley with a magnificent lake. The modern streets have noble buildings, and the ancient narrow bazaars remind one of Cairo. The Dargah, or shrine of the Mohammedan Khwaja Sahib, stands at the end of a long broad bazaar; and behind, to the north-east, rises Taragar, a hill about one thousand feet

TOMB AT ALWÁR, RAJPUTANA.

above the valley, on the lower part of which are the remains of a Jain temple, converted into a mosque, called "the mosque of two days and a half," because it probably just took this length of time to knock off the heads of the pillars on the columns, and to destroy the memorials of the former worship. The roof is supported by four rows of graceful pillars, all carved in patterns up to the very top; and the ceiling is covered with various designs, the lotus flower being frequent, indicating its connection with Buddhism. In Ajmere are the winter quarters of the Government Agent for

Rajputana. Mayo College is intended for the education of the upper classes belonging to the various native states.

The railway now brings us northwards eighty miles from Ajmere to JAIPUR, one of the most enlightened of the Rajputana states. The city dates from 1730, when the government was removed from the old capital Amber, five miles distant. Here there is a collegiate institution for the training of native youths, and a school of art in connection with it. The houses are stuccoed and painted in pink and white, and the public gardens are tastefully laid out. The neighbourhood abounds in game. The streets are wide, the houses two stories high, the second story having only loopholes, through which the women can look without being seen. The dresses of the people are gay and varied, the colours brilliant. The view of the old town of Amber from the Durbar Hall is very beautiful. When the Prince of Wales was at Jaipur, the Mohammedan festival of the Moharrem was celebrated with great pomp. This festival is in memory of the martyrdom of the sons of Ali, the immediate descendants of the Prophet, who were put to death by rival claimants to the headship of Islam. The dress of the women in Rajputana is thus described by a lady writer: "The Hindu women wear petticoats; the Mohammedans rather tight trousers, with scarfs of brilliantly-coloured muslin over their heads and bodies; many bracelets of glass, silver or lead, reaching nearly to the elbow, with an armlet above; earrings all round the ears, seven, ten, or more; large anklets of silver or lead; toe-rings that jingle as they shuffle along, their feet bare, of course." On the borders of Jaipur is the Sambar Salt Lake; and salt is manufactured by evaporation all over this part of Rajputana. Now salt is a Government monopoly in India, and, to levy the tax, we have actually put a fence of prickly pear round Rajputana. The Government, says Mr. Princep, have been trying to come to an agreement with Ram Sing in the matter of his salt, and he was invited to Simla to discuss the business. The Viceroy, Lord Lytton, with extreme friendliness said, taking his hand in both his, "Maharajah, if there is anything I can do for you, please mention it." "There *is* one thing," answered Ram Sing, "please not to mention the word *salt;*" by which reply the Rajah got the better of the Viceroy.

From Jaipur northwards, a hundred miles by rail, we reach ALWÁR, on the way to Delhi, which stands two thousand feet above the sea-level, with tooth-like hills of quartz and slate, crowned with forts. The Rajah's palace faces these hills, and from a window at the back you look out upon a tank, on the opposite side of which is a series of small temples, and on the left, or south, the tomb of Baktawar Sing, erected within the present century, of white marble upon a platform of rose-coloured sandstone. It affords a good specimen of the foliated arch. The singular dome terminates in a massive stone pinnacle. On the north there rises a fantastic hill a thousand feet high, with blocks of marble interspersed among trees, and crowned by a castle. The whole scene, in its still calm, the buildings mirrored in the water below, looks so unlike a bit of the common world, so picture-like, as seen out of that small opening, that one almost expects to see it disappear as in a panorama, and another picture take its place.

SCULPTURED CAVE IN GWALIOR.

The story is told that the Government Agent proposed to plant an avenue of pipal trees (*Ficus religiosa*), considered sacred by the Hindus, on either side the road in front of the shops; but the *Bunniahs*, or native shopkeepers, one and all declared that if this were done they would not take the shops;

and when pressed for a reason, replied that "it was because they could not tell untruths or swear falsely under their shade," adding, "and how can we carry on business otherwise?" The force of this argument seems to have been acknowledged, as the point was yielded, and other trees have been planted instead. The pipal is regarded as occupied by the god Brahma, and it is sometimes invested with the sacred thread, as if it were a real person. The planting of it is accompanied by a religious ceremony, and the prayer offered, "O Vishnu! grant that for planting this tree I may continue as many years in heaven as this tree shall remain growing in the earth." It is never injured, cut down, or burnt by devout Hindus; but the proximity of the tree does not always guarantee truthfulness. The aborigines of the Central Provinces are called Gonds, a very peculiar race, with black skin, thick lips, and flat nose, and wêaring for clothing only the loin cloth. They are of dirty habits, tatooed, and addicted to drinking. As to their religion, Dr. Hunter tells us that "they worship cholera and small-pox, and to appease the wrath of these divinities they offer sacrifices; cleaning their villages, they place the sweepings on a road or track, in the hope that some traveller will be infected, and so convey the disease away into another village."

East of Rajputana is the CENTRAL INDIA AGENCY, with a population of eight millions, embracing no less than seventy different states, the chief of which are Gwalior, Indore, Bhopal, Rewah, and Bundelcund. They all formed part of the extensive Mahratta kingdom, which stretched from Gwalior as far south as Goa. The Mahrattas are supposed to have been among the original tribes of India, driven south by the Aryans. They were a bold and industrious race, husbandmen, for the most part, strong and self-reliant; and they appear in history first under Sivaji, who united the several tribes in a valiant crusade against the Mogul conquerors of India, and maintained the conflict with unflinching courage till his death in 1680. The Mahrattas are born horsemen; they ride sturdy ponies, and show great skill and bravery as skirmishers. They not only checked, but in effect subdued the Mohammedan power, which declined from the time of Sivaji. In his rule the Brahman element was strong, and to the Peishwas the military authority was subservient. One of these Peishwas raised the Scindia family of Mahrattas to the highest place as military leaders, and under them the Mahrattas were found to be formidable foes, even by well-equipped English troops. Their capital is still GWALIOR, with its huge isolated rock, three hundred feet high with perpendicular sides, and a mile and a half long, impregnable against any native force. On the summit is King Pal, a fortress and palace in one, as if growing out of the rock; and farther on the huge temple of Adinath, a striking specimen of Jain architecture. In the centre is the Vihara Temple, conspicuous from afar, dating probably from the eleventh century, and now a hundred and twenty feet high, though probably it was in its complete state much higher. On the west of the plateau the rock is split into a deep, narrow gorge, full of curious carvings on either side; chiefly colossal figures with sphinx-like faces representing Adinath, thirty-five feet high, and other Tirthankars, or Jain deities. Above each statue is a canopy of richly-carved stone. Jainism prevails in these districts, and was by some viewed as an offshoot of Buddhism; but it is now generally regarded as having an independent origin, dating back as far as Buddhism itself. It lays great stress upon the doctrine of transmigration, and care for animal life is carried to an

SACRED HILL, SONAGHUR.

absurd length. The Jains retain caste distinctions, and are divided into two sects, the "clothed in white," and the "sky-clothed." Their sacred books are called Agamas. Though they dissent from the Veda, they call themselves Hindus. They pay great reverence to any Jina, or "conquering saint," who by long discipline aims at Divine perfection.

BUNDELCUND, which lies to the east, is the classic land of brigandism, and in its sombre forests was born the terrible religion of the Thugs. It is one of the least known parts of India. Its capital is Duttiah, and to the west of this city stands the palace of Birsing-Deo, a square block of building (see p. 185), each side of which is a hundred yards long and ninety feet high. The whole is of granite built upon a vaulted terrace. The rooms are large, but badly lighted. Everything is sombre and massive, like a keep, and it is abandoned to the bats and the owls. Its gardens lead down to the lake, which, with its tombs opposite, presents a very striking and interesting picture. One of the most famous places of pilgrimage for the Jains of Central India is Sonaghur, "the golden mountain." On the road from Dattia the hills present the appearance of broken pyramidal blocks of granite, and some like cromlechs and Druidical remains in single huge blocks. Many of these monoliths are worshipped as *lingas*, and are smeared with red ochre. Sonaghur (p. 191) rises in strange and picturesque outline, a granite hill, with large loose masses of primitive rock, among which stand from eighty to a hundred temples of various shapes and sizes, with bulbous domes, and copied in some degree from Moslem art. There is no vegetation; the rocks are bare, and look as if they would fall upon and crush the buildings, which are inhabited only by a few Jain monks. A pretty little village, half hidden in trees, lies at the foot of the hill.

One of the most interesting collections of Buddhist remains is found at SANCHI, in the neighbourhood of BHILSA, and in the district of BHOPAL. The small village of Sanchi is on the ridge of a sandstone hill five miles from Bhilsa and twenty miles north-east from the town of Bhopal. The hill is flat-topped and isolated, with a steep cliff eastward. Its height is three hundred feet, the rock is light red sandstone, and the ruins are on the top. They lie so remote from the sweep of Mohammedan and British conquest that they have escaped the damage and destruction that have befallen many Indian monuments of antiquity. They consist mainly of topes or stupas, *i.e.* huge hemispherical mounds usually raised in early Buddhism to mark the place of relics or graves. Of these topes there are upwards of twenty-five, larger or smaller, within a distance of ten miles. We know from historical sources, the Mahadeva in particular, that Asoka, the Buddhist king, grandson of the great Chandra Gupta, tarried some time at Besnagar, close to Sanchi, and there married Devi, the daughter of the chief, by whom he had twin sons, Ujenio and Mahinda (who went to Ceylon), and a daughter. There is also a record of a farewell visit paid by Mahinda to his royal mother at Sanchi.

THE MOHARREM IN BHOPAL.

No doubt, therefore, the topes at Sanchi were raised by Asoka or Mahinda; and perhaps the great tope may be a monument in remembrance of Asoka's wife, the royal mother of Mahinda. It has been dug into, and is found solid, nothing but bricks laid in mud, save the layers of smooth stones covered with plaster on the outside surface. No relics have been discovered. Topes were built by forced labour, the foundations being trodden firm by elephants. This tope is almost hemispherical, a hundred and six feet in diameter at the base, and forty-two feet in height. The hemisphere stands upon a base twelve feet high and forming a path seven feet wide, with a staircase up to it, round the tope, where it is supposed processions used to walk on festival occasions. The circumference of the building, measured round the base, is five hundred and fifty feet. It is surrounded by a stone railing, the stones, nine feet high, being morticed and fitted like those at Stonehenge; and there are four gateways, facing the four points of the compass. The red sandstone has been used for all the topes; where hardness was required and in the gateways, a fine white sandstone from a place three miles off was employed. Three of these gateways were standing thirty years ago, but one was knocked down by some clumsy Englishmen, and only two, the east gate and the north gate, now remain. The east gate has been modelled for South Kensington Museum; the frontispiece to this chapter is of the Northern Gate, which is the finest and most elaborate. Supposing that the tope itself was raised B.C. 250, inscriptions on each rail show that it was the gift of a different individual, and thus the whole circle may have taken a century or more to erect. The gateways, too, were added at intervals—the oldest dating about A.D. 20, the northern next, and afterwards the other two. Mr. Fergusson considers that the four gateways may have been added to the tope during the first century of the Christian era. The northern gateway is the largest; its height is thirty-five feet, and its extreme width is twenty feet. Two vertical monoliths eighteen feet high support a third placed horizontally and morticed in like woodwork, and somewhat resembling the Torii in Japan. Above this two small blocks support a second horizontal monolith, and again two blocks support the topmost horizontal stone. The whole is elaborately carved back and front with sculptures representing scenes (it is supposed) from the life of Buddha; but if so the scenes must be from Buddha's life before he became an ascetic, for drinking and love-making are portrayed, several nude female figures are introduced, and images of the goddess Devi, the wife of Vishnu. The emblems on the top closely resemble those of Dharma and Juggernaut.

THE GAIKWAR ELEPHANT IN THE GREAT SOWARI AT BARODA.

BOMBAY PRESIDENCY.

BHORE GHAT RAILWAY.

BOMBAY PRESIDENCY.

JABALPUR, AJANTA, AND ELURA — BOMBAY — CAVES OF ELEPHANTA, KENNERY, KARLI — MATAERAN — POONA — MAHABLESHWAR — SURAT — BARODA — KUTCH —SINDE.

THE tourist across India from Allahabad to Bombay, or *vice versâ*, usually breaks the long railway journey (eight hundred and fifty miles and thirty-six hours) at JABALPUR, a large and flourishing city in the Central Provinces, in order to visit the Marble Rocks, one of the most remarkable scenes of natural beauty to be found in India. Jabalpur is two hundred and thirty miles from Allahabad and a thousand feet above the sea; it is overlooked by a range of hills, consisting of granite, gneiss, hornblende, dolomite, and always covered with verdure. The Marble Rocks are eleven miles from Jabalpur; and on the way you pass Mudden Mahal, with curious hills commanding an extensive view of Jabalpur and the country round, and crowned with a ruined temple on the top of a huge black boulder, while about the base are numerous tanks and mango groves. At the Marble Rocks the deep blue Narbada for two miles flows between two radiant snow-white walls a hundred feet in height. The river, now entering the gorge with a leap, has excavated this deep channel for itself, and can be traversed in a flat-bottomed boat, which is rowed or poled along as far as the cascade. The rocks rise precipitously from the water, and are in parts extremely white, seamed by veins of dark green or black volcanic rock. The boat passes through the gradually contracting gorge, amid the hum of bees, the chattering of monkeys, and the rustling of forest leaves. Above the rocks the river is a hundred yards broad; here it is compressed into some twenty yards; it has a great depth, and glides very smoothly. When a full strong light from sun or moon is thrown upon the rocks above, the combined effect of the marble and its reflection is quite dazzling. The play of light forms a striking contrast with the deep hues of the waters; by moonlight the rocks look ghost-like and mysterious. But the place is not free from danger. High up above you hang from the cliffs the semicircular combs of bees, which infest the gorge, and which, if disturbed by the firing of a gun or otherwise, swarm down upon the intruders, and there is no means of avoiding their cruel stings. Nevertheless the natives, by means of bamboo ladders suspended from the cliffs, manage at night to smother the bees with torches, and to rob the honey. On the summit of a low hill overlooking the Marble Rocks there are several Hindu Sivoid temples, and the Hindus still hold annually a religious gathering and a fair, attended by thousands during the moonlight of November.

In the neighbourhood of Jabalpur are the Mopani coal-fields and mines of hæmatite ore; but the amount of coal raised is not more than about a thousand tons per month, and even when sold at ten rupees a ton barely covers working expenses. In the Bombay Presidency English coal is used, and of course the prices are very high. Few stations in India can show such majestic mango-trees as Jabalpur; and it is remarkable for its pine-apples. Here also the *sâl*, a tree whose habit is to occupy, where it grows at all, the whole area to the exclusion of others, is found to rule supreme. Its seeds have a marvellous power of self-propagation, sprouting immediately on reaching the ground. It is almost the only evergreen tree in India. Many of the young forests of *sâl* resemble more the regularly tended saplings of an English plantation than self-sown trees. The timber of the *sâl*, if inferior to the teak for some purposes, is superior for others, and it is almost the only timber tree of Upper India. Singly the *sâl* is a little formal in outline, and possesses a fine firm appearance, from its horizontal branches. It has bright leaves like broad lance-heads, and straight tapering stem with grey and deeply-fissured bark. Its great charm, however, resides in the fresh cool aspect of the clumps and belts in which it chiefly grows. The bamboo thickets of the higher hills, with their light feathery foliage, beautifully supplement the heavier masses of the sâl that climb their skirts. The graciousness of nature in furnishing such plentiful shade cannot but be admired. Just at the time when the face of the country begins to quiver in the fierce sun and burning blasts of April, the banyan and peepul figs and the ever-present mango throw out a fresh crop of leaves; those of the banyan being then, moreover, charged with a thick milky juice that forms an impenetrable non-conductor to the sun's rays.

These are in substance the observations of the late Captain Forsyth, who spent a considerable time in the Narbada Valley. While a keen observer of nature, he was an ardent sportsman, and has left us some interesting facts relating to the TIGER, the inhabitant of the Indian jungle, and the devastator of the country in days gone by. Though tiger-hunting is inferior, as a mere exercise or an effort of skill, to some other pursuits, yet it furnishes a test of coolness and nerve; and there is an excitement unsurpassed in attacking an animal before whom every other beast of the forest quails, and unarmed man is helpless as the mouse under the paw of a cat. It is difficult to get information from natives as to the whereabouts of tigers. The hunter and his train of overbearing, swindling servants are shunned by the poor inhabitants. The tiger himself is, in fact, far more endurable than those who, encamping against him, demand grain and other supplies, and force the natives to beat for the tiger, with a considerable chance of getting killed, and very little chance of being paid for their services. The native, moreover, regards the tiger as a sort of protector, destroying the wild animals which feed upon the crops. The confirmed man-eater, however, is a deadly foe, and much real courage is shown in tiger-hunting, when it is not carried on in large multitudinous companies.

Tigers are now very much rarer to meet with than they once were, when Government offered a reward for each tiger's head sufficient to maintain a peasant's family in comfort for three months. All this is now changed, and it is a frequent complaint that one can so seldom get a shot at a tiger. The only animal, says Dr. W. W. Hunter, that has defied the energy of the British official is the snake. The ascertained number of persons who died from snake-bite in 1875 was seventeen thousand, out of a total of twenty-one thousand three hundred and ninety-one killed by snakes and all other wild animals.

Leaving Jabalpur, the great Indian Peninsula Railway conveys us through the picturesque valley of the Narbada, wild, woody, uncultivated and thinly peopled. The railway stations are like oases, few and distant from each other, bright with flowers and well supplied with refreshments, in the midst of jungle. At Khandwa, the branch line to Indore turns northwards towards Delhi, opening up a very fertile and productive country for cotton, tobacco, and opium. Indore itself is an ill-built city with a few mosques, but with little to demand the tourist's attention. The large military cantonment of Mhow, about twelve miles south-west from Indore, is quite a European town. Fifty miles farther on along the main line, we come to the branch for Nagpur, a straggling city in a swampy hollow, but much improved by tanks and watercourses, and the largest city in the Central Provinces. Nine miles from Nagpur is the cantonment of Kamthi.

In order to visit the famous caves of Ajanta and Elura, we take a slow train from Bhosawal to Pachora, from which the caves are about thirty-two miles distant. Visitors from Bombay usually leave the train at Nandgaon. The Buddhist caves at Ajanta, in a deep glen, penetrating far into the mountain, are twenty-nine in number, with fresco paintings on the walls and ceilings, illustrative of the religious and social life of the people when Buddhism still flourished. None of the caves are high, and there is nothing imposing connected with them. The principal object within is either a Chaitya, a Dagoba, *i.e.*, relic-shrine, or an image of Buddha. In some of the rock-temples here, as may be seen in the illustration, the older Buddhism had disappeared, and Brahmanism had begun to re-assert its sway. Instead of paintings, we find sculptures and images, not of Buddha only, but of Hindu gods and goddesses. It is supposed that this revolution in religious belief was commenced before the fourth century of our era, and indeed that images of Buddha were hardly known in India nor worshipped after the seventh century. The series of excavations extends along the face of a tall cliff for a distance of five hundred yards; and some of the caverns are a hundred feet deep and forty wide. Below them is a beautiful waterfall, which bounds from rock to rock from a height of three hundred feet, and the glen is green and shady with forest trees and numerous creepers.

BUDDHA.

We pursue our way from Ajanta by road to Aurangabad, near which is the far-famed fortress of Doulatabad, an extraordinary hill, consisting of a huge conical rock five hundred feet high, and cut perpendicular all round for a height of forty yards. A winding passage inside leads first to a chamber and then to the summit, which is occupied by the fortress. Leaving this place, we ascend the Ghât or mountain-ridge to Roza, where on the plateau we see several Mohammedan tombs, one of which has been converted into a bungalow. Descending the Ghât on the other side, we reach the caves of ELURA, situated near the base of a crescent-shaped range of hills six hundred feet high. There are thirty caves, of which ten are Buddhist, towards the south, the most ancient; fourteen Brahmanical, in the centre, the most elaborate; and six Jaina northwards. They are cut in greenstone-rock, and extend a mile and a half along the amphitheatre. Cascades fall in front of the caves, and the base of the mountain is fringed with brush-wood and trees. The best time for a visit is after the rains, when the country is green and the waterfalls full. The Kailas, or Paradise Cave, is the most wonderful. Within a pit is an entire temple cut out of the solid rock, a monolithic Brahmanical temple of the eighth century, with columns and walls elaborately carved, and a pyramidal spire over the shrine. Dr. Wilson, of Bombay, when he visited this cave, preached the gospel in it to a congregation of thirty natives. "Some of our auditors," he says, "pointed to the magnificent arches and stupendous figures around us, as the very works of God's own hand; but we pointed them to the marks of the instrument of the mason, to the innumerable proofs of decay every-where exhibited, and to the unsuitableness, absurdity, and impiety of the representations. They could not resist our appeal. Little did the formers of this wonderful structure anticipate an event of this kind. We were probably the first messengers of peace who have declared within it the claims of Jehovah."

Resuming our railway journey towards Bombay at Nandgaum, we make another halt sixty miles farther on at NASSICK, which lies at the foot of the great Western Ghâts on their eastern side, where the Godavery rises. Nassick is called the Benares of Western India, and is pleasantly situated on the banks of the Godavery, which here is broad but shallow, and lined with temples. The country is fertile and well-wooded; the town is eighteen hundred feet above the sea, and its advantages are so great that Sir G. Campbell seriously proposed to make it the capital of India. Its population is thirty-five thousand, including ten thousand Brahmans. There is a very pleasant excursion to Gungapore, eight miles farther up the Godavery, where there are nine temples and a pretty waterfall; but the chief sight is the Buddhist caves of Pandu Lena, running round a conical hill five miles from the town. They are seventeen in number, and were excavated in the fourth century of our era, though from an inscription over the entrance of one of them it seems to bear date B.C. 129. The mountains round are very majestic, but everything is so associated with the reigning superstition, that one of these is called the Bed of Rama, its summit being a table-land. The river is an object of great attraction, and besides the great Rama-Kunda, or pool for bathing, there are eleven other pools, sacred to some of the gods. The Church Mission has established here an industrial settlement, called Sharanpur, or "city of refuge," where there is a Christian congregation, schools, an orphanage, and an asylum.

And now resuming our journey along the main line, we see our way blocked up by rocks ahead; and the apparently impassable barrier of the Western Ghâts, which run parallel to the west coast of India northwards from the Nilgiri Hills, rises in all its majesty before us. But the iron horse gradually winds its way snake-like, now round this shoulder, and now across that ravine, till at length we are on the top of the ridge of the Thull Ghât. The line curves round precipices like the worm of a screw, while you look out on one side of the carriage at the overhanging rocks, and on the other see below the deep ravine with its roaring torrent. It is a noble piece of engineering. The incline is nine miles long, with many zigzags, and thirteen tunnels. The sharpest curve is one of seventeen chains radius, and the maximum gradient is one in thirty-seven. There are fifteen bridges and six viaducts. The descent down the sea-face of the Thull Ghât is very fine; lofty cliffs, green slopes, wooded gorges, roaring streams, forests of palm and teak, aromatic groves—all combining to present a picture of grandeur and loveliness. At length we reach the Konkan, the level strip of country intervening between the mountains and the sea, and passing through Tanna, on the Island of Salsette, we arrive at the terminus in Bombay.

How grateful is the sweet smell of the sea and its refreshing breeze after three thousand miles of inland travel and several weeks of inland sojourn in North India! At home in Britain we never lose the bracing freshness which the sea imparts to the stiff or gentle gales, because in any direction the sea is not far off; but when we cross, for example, the American continent from New York to San Francisco, or still more, when we make the journey from Calcutta, through the plains of Bengal and the North-West Provinces to Karáchi or Bombay, the days or weeks of inland sojourn and travel amid arid plains and over scorching plateaux make one long for the pleasant sight of the sea and the refreshing odour of the ocean breeze. And these breezes, BOMBAY—"fair haven," as the names signifies—enjoys in double measure, for it is a city built upon an island, or chain of islands, branching out southwards from the mainland, and enclosing a splendid harbour of forty square miles. The fort was ceded by the Portuguese in 1661 to Charles II., who handed it over to the East India Company in 1668 for an annual rent of "ten pounds in gold." Owing to the increased growth of Indian cotton, and still more to the opening of the Suez Canal, Bombay has rapidly grown during the present century into a city of seven hundred thousand inhabitants. Of these four hundred thousand are Hindus, one hundred and fifty thousand Mohammedans, fifty thousand Parsis, and the remainder Jains, Eurasians, and Europeans. The variety of nationality and costume is perhaps more striking here than anywhere else in India. Crowds of coolies, or labourers, with their dark skins, turbaned heads, and the strip of cloth around their loins; native women, graceful in figure and features, decked out in many colours—crimson and white and yellow, orange, green, and blue—with heavy bracelets on arms and ankles; Parsis, with white garments and dark towering hats,

STREET IN BOMBAY.

and Mohammedans, proud and stately, all bustling along beneath the tropical sun, and in an atmosphere transparent and bright, present a scene most picturesque and exhilarating. The native town stretches northwards, and here is the centre of trade. There is, however, no distinctively European quarter in Bombay, Englishmen and natives having their offices side by side. Southwards, beyond the Green, is the Fort, now no longer a fort, but an esplanade with levelled ramparts and with noble buildings—the new Secretariat, the new Post Office, the High Court, the University Library and Tower, all European in their style. Beyond these is the promontory of Lower Colaba, with mainly a seafaring population.

To one coming for the first time into Bombay from the sea, it is a new sensation to be in this Asiatic atmosphere, surrounded and waited upon by soft-footed Hindus, who glide about noiselessly like cats, watching every

COTTON WEIGHING.

look, eager to anticipate every wish; indeed, you cannot enter the hotel without a dozen servants rising to their feet and making salaams with profound reverence as you pass. But one soon learns to accept these obeisances, and to play the English grandee. Native service in India is so cheap that every Englishman has his attendants; and no sooner does the youth, who at home was wont to do everything for himself, set foot here, than he discovers that by virtue of his belonging to the conquering race he can hold his head high, smoke at leisure, and be waited upon by mild Hindus, making obeisance to him from the moment he rises in the morning till he is asleep at night. Nay, his servant, like a faithful dog, lies in readiness on the mat outside his door all through the night, and two others are pulling the punkah through the silent hours over sahib's head. He falls moreover into the habit of drinking "pegs," as drams of spirits with or without soda water are called. The name arose from the mode of marking, by pegs opposite his name, each soldier's allowance as he got it twice daily in the barrack canteen. An old officer returning from the country said to me, "I know no worse school for a young man than India. I have two nephews who have inherited land in Oude; I am trying to persuade their guardians to sell the land there, and to buy farms for them in New Zealand or America. There they must learn industry and self-dependence. Here in India they learn to be haughty, idle, imperious, self-indulgent." This is the temptation, and this is the threatening danger; for the Hindu is not slow to perceive that by hard taxation he really pays for the pomp and retinue of English officials, their incomes from the Viceroy downwards being practically drawn from the sweat of his brow. But to the prevailing arrogance there are many noble exceptions, men who fear God, who respect the Hindu as a man, not merely regard him as a brute; who fulfil the duty for which they are paid by the people with conscientiousness and kindness; who eschew "pegs," and live temperate and pure lives; who treat the people with justice and humanity. These men are our strength in India.

The favourite suburb for the wealthy is Malabar Hill, a lofty ridge about five hundred feet high, which stretches as a separate promontory for two miles out to sea in a south-westerly direction. This thickly wooded ridge commands glorious views of the city and the ocean. It is dotted over with bungalows, shaded with palms, and embowered in tropical foliage. Here at evening, on the broad verandahs, the merchant or official, stretched in his long bamboo chair, can enjoy the cool ocean breeze. The Government Bungalow is at the extreme point, and from it the drive of five miles down the slope and along the beach leads to the Apollo Bunder, where the fashion of Bombay drives in the afternoon until sunset, and gathers to the music of the band. The equipages of the wealthy Parsís and of the English residents sweep along, with trails of native footmen.

The Parsís, who are descendants of the ancient Persians, and who settled at Surat a thousand years ago, are now an intelligent and enterprising community, rivalling Europeans in opulence. Much of the mercantile business of the East is in their hands. They speak English with fluency, and in their schools English is universally taught. As to religion, they are the followers of Zoroaster, whose precepts in the Zendavesta are summed up thus: "Good thoughts," "good words," "good deeds." Theoretically they claim to be monotheists, but they adore the four elements, fire, air, earth, and water; they will not contaminate earth by any burial, nor fire by cremation. In their own cemetery on Malabar Hill are five mysterious stone receptacles for their dead, about eight yards high and twenty wide, called "towers of silence." Each tower possesses usually an extraordinary coping, not of dead stone but of living vultures. There they sit motionless with their heads pointed inwards. Inside each tower are a number of stone receptacles, like the spokes of a wheel pointing inwards, open at the top and sloping towards the centre, where is a deep well with charcoal and sand below. When a funeral occurs the body is brought to the bottom of the incline leading to the tower, and here the mourners retire, leaving the bearers to advance with their burden. The corpse is silently conveyed into the interior, laid uncovered in one of the open stone receptacles, and left there. Scarcely is the door closed when the vultures swoop down upon the body, and in five minutes the satiated birds fly back and settle down again upon the parapet. Meanwhile the mourners change their clothes, leaving their funeral garments behind them. The dry skeleton is afterwards placed in the centre well, gradually to disappear below. A Parsi merchant with whom I travelled for several days strongly vindicated this use of birds of prey, as reverential to the four sacred elements, as less revolting than worms, and as best contributing to the health of the living. The best account of Parseeism is Dr. Wilson's work *The Parsi Religion.* Under his instruction several Parsis embraced Christianity, and two are now ordained missionaries.

Besides the Grant Medical Hospital, so well known for its efficiency, may be named the Panjrapul, a hospital for diseased and decrepit animals. This has been founded and is supported mainly by the Jains, with whom tenderness for animal life is a distinguishing tenet. They are most careful lest they should tread on or crush any insect, or by accident swallow the tiniest mite. They strain the water which they drink (a wise precaution for sanitary reasons), and they will not eat or drink in the dark, lest they should inadvertently swallow life. This care arises from their belief that life everywhere, whether in trees or animals or man, is one and the same; they contend for the *identity* of life in all kinds of existences. In the hospital all sick or maimed animals are treated, from the elephant to the dog; even fleas and other vermin are carefully nursed. Crows, cows, monkeys, serpents are regarded as more or less pervaded by Divinity, and any noxious insect or reptile may be an incarnation of a deceased relative. The Jina is "a conquering saint," and the principal point in the creed of Jainas is the reverence paid to holy men who have attained perfection. One way of winning perfection is to found a hospital for broken-down animals or to build a new temple.

Having hired a steam-launch, we started one beautiful morning for the island of ELEPHANTA, six miles south-east of Bombay, and after a delightful passage reached the landing-place, a long narrow pier, in an hour and a half. A stone pathway and steps lead up to the famous caves, where the custodian furnishes you with a ticket of admission; and with the guide-book you can decipher all that is to be seen. Three massive columns cut out of the solid rock divide the entrance, and support a huge overhanging cliff mantled

ENTRANCE TO THE CAVES OF ELEPHANTA.

with verdure and draped with flowering creepers. The regularity of the pillars, which run in parallel lines, and the coarseness of the workmanship, indicate the comparative lateness of the work. The great cave is about one hundred and thirty feet deep, and equally wide, hollowed out of trap rock, huge pillars being left in rows to support the roof, which is about twenty feet high. This is a very fair specimen of the rock temples of the Hindus. Facing you in the distance, at the back of the cave as you enter, is a fine colossal cutting of the Hindu trinity, Brahma the creator in the centre, Vishnu the preserver on your left, Siva the destroyer on your right. The three faces are combined as if in three huge heads, and the carving of the head-dresses is very carefully executed. On every hand huge bas-reliefs stare passively from the rocky walls around, and represent Siva in various forms, with his wife Parvati. The fact that all the designs in the cavern clearly refer to Siva only, has led to the conclusion that the entire temple was dedicated to him, under the name Trimurti, and that the three colossal heads in the centre represent him only, in three different characters: the centre being in feature calm and benevolent, that on the left merry and joyous, that on the right fierce and revengeful. On the west side of this monster hall is the most holy place, wherein there rises an immense *linga* shrine, the emblem of the creative powers of the universe, and the most frequent, indeed, the universal object of idolatry throughout India. Around are giant Brahmans in stone placed as guards; and hither, in the days when worship was celebrated in the temple, the costliest offerings were brought. We pause before this in horror and sadness, as we think of the age which could revel in the beliefs which these figures embody. On the east side a panel depicts the birth of the elephant-headed god of wisdom, Ganesh. Here, too, is what is called the Lions' Cave, on account of two colossal lions in basalt which were discovered in some excavations, and have been placed here. Again you have Siva as an ascetic, and Siva in the dance. In fact, there is quite a theogony here. The flat ponderous roof of mountain, the pillars as if pressed down and bulging out with its weight, the sombre gloom pervading the recesses, and the weird and fantastic carvings on every hand, give to the place an air of mysteriousness and gloom. If civilized man views it with amazement, and is impressed with its grandeur, no wonder that devout and credulous Hindus once regarded it with awe as the dwelling-place of an omnipotent and relentless deity. This huge and gloomy rock-temple dates as far back as the ninth century of our era. Outside, the island is fertile, romantic, and hilly—a delightful contrast, as the temple of the Almighty, with the dark idol shrine within; and boys brought for sale beautifully-coloured flies and pendent birds' nests. The excursion to and from Elephanta is easily accomplished in a day, and there is no pleasanter one in the neighbourhood of Bombay.

What the caves of Elephanta were for Brahmanism the Kennery caves, in the opposite direction, were for Buddhism; and the visitor at Bombay has within a day's excursion a very interesting specimen of both these classes of cave architecture. The KENNERY caves are six miles from Tanna railway station. They are almost a hundred in number, and are hollowed out of a large hill in a tract of thick forest. The pillars of the great cave are somewhat like those of Elephanta; but in the Vihara, which is about forty yards long, there is a colossal figure of Buddha on either side.

GROTTO AT KENNERY.

Flights of steps lead up to the top of the hill, which commands an extensive view, and here are a number of smaller caves, all with indications of Buddhist worship. Traces of plaster and painting are observable, supposed to be the work of the Buddhists when driven from Karli. Many of these rock temples were no doubt originally natural caves. Being carved in the living rock, and not built up with stone, they remain just as they were at

BAS-RELIEFS, GATEWAY OF KARLI.

the beginning, and have not been altered or repaired. The Kennery caves bear date about the fifth century of our era. Dr. Wilson enumerates no fewer than thirty-seven groups of these cave temples in the Bombay Presidency, the greater number being of Buddhist origin. Those of Elura were the first, then followed the Karli caves, and the latest imitations of them are the Jain excavations. Of all these rock-temples the finest perhaps are those of KARLI, about eighty miles by railway from Bombay. The great Chaitya cave here is hewn in the face of a precipice, two-thirds up the side of a thickly-wooded hill. In front of it stands the Lion Pillar, a monolith of exquisite architectural proportions, with four stone lions back to back in its capital. The doorway is through a screen carved with colossal figures. The

INTERIOR OF GREAT DAGOBA OF KARLI.

cave itself looks like an oblong church, with a nave and side aisles. It is forty yards long by twelve yards wide, and has a semicircular apse behind the shrine. The roof is dome-like, ornamented by a series of wooden rafters and resting on forty pillars, each having a richly-moulded capital on which kneel two elephants, each bearing two figures. The chaitya, or dagoba, is a dome on a circular drum surmounted by the remains of a wooden *chattar*, or umbrella. The only light which is admitted from without comes from a horseshoe window, and falls on this object with great effect. The sculptures represent the aboriginal tribes doing obeisance to Buddha. From inscriptions that have been deciphered, the date of this Buddhist temple is about B.C. 78. There is nothing in ancient Buddhist architecture that so closely resembles mediæval Christian building. Not the least wonderful here are the reservoirs of ever-cool water, some of them of great depth and cut out of the living rock. The finest cathedrals of Europe do not always excite such emotions as the Karli temple dedicated to Gautama Buddha. It bears this inscription: "By the victorious and most exalted king, this rock mansion has been established, the most excellent in India."

Leaving Bombay by the Great Indian Peninsula Railway, two hours will find us at Narel, fifty-three miles distance, and within six miles of MATHERAN, a healthy hill station about two thousand five hundred feet above the sea, where we find ourselves away from the noise and heat of the city, in the midst of lovely scenery and a pure and buoyant atmosphere, with the scent of wild flowers and the songs of birds. There are fine views of the Ghâts from Garbut Point, and Panorama Point commands the wide expanse of the Konkan, with the sea beyond. On the east of the hill is a noble grove, where magnificent trees are to be seen festooned by gigantic creepers. Many Bombay merchants come out hither daily during the hot months. Resuming our railway journey, we now ascend the BHORE GHÂT, which is two thousand feet above the sea level. Here the mountains are precipitously scarped, and the railway wends its way, round precipices and in zigzags, to the summit of the tremendous ravine. At one point the angle is so sharp that trains cannot turn, and they reverse their direction on a level terrace. This range was considered the key of the Deccan in the early wars of the English with the Mahrattas, and a proposal was made to fortify it. Better far is the traversing of it first by an excellent road, and next by a railway, which surmounts the barrier, and brings Poona within six hours of Bombay.

POONA is one of the old capitals of the Mahratta, or "Great Kingdom," as the word signifies, the other two capitals being Satura and Kolhapore. Here the Peishwa ruled till his defeat in 1818; and since that time the city has not been so flourishing. It is situated in a wide-stretching treeless plain, and is divided into seven quarters, called by the seven days of the week. The inhabitants are chiefly Hindus, and there are many Brahmans, fat and sleek, to be seen in the streets. The shrine of Parvati is on an eminence overlooking the town. Here are the Government English Schools, the Sanscrit College, and the military headquarters for Western India. Seventy miles journey south by a good but hilly road brings us to MAHABLESHWAR, a glorious sanatorium, four thousand seven hundred feet above the sea, and the Simla of the Bombay Presidency. It is now more easily approached by steam from Bombay to Dasgaum, and thence by the new Ghât road through Poladpur and Warra. Perhaps the best description of this charming resort is from the pen of the late Rev. Dr. John Wilson, who had a bungalow here for many years. He says: "I am at present sojourning on the most lovely spot that you can imagine. The scenery around is the grandest, the most beautiful, and the most sublime which I have yet witnessed during my earthly wanderings, extensive though they have been. The Mahableshwar is part of the Great Western Ghâts, and four thousand seven hundred feet high, a loftiness surpassing the highest of Caledonia's mountains. The vegetation partakes of the magnificence of the tropics, but is enchanting to the dwellers in the climes of the sun, as in some respects resembling that of our beloved native land. The *matériel* of the heights is of the trap formation, which, by its basaltic masses and columns and precipitous scarps, affords the most wonderful and diversified specimens of Nature's architecture, and by its valleys

MAHABLESHWAR.

and ravines, of her gigantic excavation. The province of the Konkan, with its hills and dales, and exhaustless forests and fruitful fields, stretches below. At a distance the ocean is seen as a vast mirror of brilliancy, reflecting the glory of the sky. The clouds baffle all description. Their various and changing hues, and multifarious forms and motions, as they descend to kiss the mountain brow, or remain above as our fleecy mantle, or interpose between us and the luminary of heaven to catch its rays, and to reveal their coloured splendour, fill the mind with the most intense delight. . . . Satara, in my opinion, is the most lovely station in our Presidency. The valley of the Yena, with its abundant cultivation, and that of the Krishna, which partly appears, and the mountains to the west, and the hills to the north and south, presenting, with their basaltic masses, and layers, and columns, and scarps, and towers, the most interesting specimens of Nature's architecture, have a very striking effect on the eye of the spectator. The fort is curiously formed on the summit of one of the highest elevations; and it is associated with all the interest and romance of Mahratti history. The native town is spacious, busy, and regular, to a degree seldom seen in this country. The camp is very agreeably situated; and the Residency has a beautiful neighbourhood."

JEWESSES, BOMBAY.

No European knew the Bombay Presidency so well as did Dr. Wilson. He went out as a missionary in the year 1829, at once set himself to master the Mahratti language, and soon became eminent as a champion of the Christian religion with Parsis, Mohammedans and Hindus. He ranked *facile princeps* among Oriental scholars, was President of the Bombay Asiatic Society, wrote several valuable treatises, and was consulted upon political questions by the highest authorities in India. He travelled through every part of the Bombay Presidency; and after a life-sojourn of forty-seven years, he died esteemed and lamented by all classes, on the 1st of December, 1875. The Free Church Institute stands a monument of his labours in the city. I went through the several class-rooms with deep interest and surprise, and addressed the senior class of native students, who spoke English fluently, and greatly astonished me with their intelligent questions. I also visited the Jews' School, in which Dr. Wilson took deep interest, for there are many *Beni-Israel*, as they are called, in

Bombay, and here are nearly a hundred Jewish children, boys and girls, learning Hebrew and English, and reading the Hebrew Bible. The American missions in Bombay date from 1813, and have been all along conducted with zeal and efficiency. Driving across the Esplanade one Saturday, I saw a large crowd of Hindus gathered at the foot of one of the statues; and in the midst of them stood the venerable Mr. Bowen, holding an open-air service, and preaching the Gospel of Christ. He, like Dr. Wilson, is a veteran in mission work, and is highly esteemed by the Hindus.

The Bombay Presidency extends southwards past the Portuguese settlement of Goa, and includes North Kanara. The first sight of Goa is magnificent, and the houses look substantial; but it is evident that little remains but the churches and some other public buildings. The view from the turrets of the Augustinian convent is magnificent. The Gairsoppa Falls, which are about three hundred and forty miles south of Bombay, in North Kanara, are reckoned among the chief wonders of India. Here the Sheravatty divides into several channels above the old capital of Gairsoppa. There are four distinct falls, but they can be seen together, and November is the best month to visit them. They are named the "Rajah," the "Roarer," the "Rocket," and "Dame Blanche." The "Rajah" falls in a single leap a depth of eight hundred feet, but the other three glide in a thick body of water down the sloping rocks.

Northwards the Bombay Presidency embraces the peninsular lands of Gujarat and Kutch, and the district called Sinde, which includes the mouths of the Indus. Taking the Bombay and Baroda line, we reach Surat (one hundred and sixty-seven miles) in eight hours, an ugly town, but famous in history, and an outpost of the Mahrattas. It was one of the first English settlements in India, and declined as Bombay supplanted it. Here there are several factories, and the place is well known for its cotton. There are in Western India at present forty-one cotton factories. The inhabitants of Surat have shown great intelligence and spirit in resisting unjust taxation. The tombs of the governors of the English and Dutch factories are immense structures, in imitation of Mohammedans, and meant to impress the natives with the greatness and wealth of the owners. The railway stations along this line are beautifully kept, and have gardens smiling with flowers. Another hundred miles are traversed in about five hours, and we reach Baroda, the capital of the Mahratta chief, called the Gaikwar, or "cowherd." The city is divided into four quarters by wide streets, meeting in the centre at a spacious market-place. The population is said to be two hundred thousand. The houses are mostly of wood, and the country around is charmingly fertile. The Gaikwar's court is a scene of great splendour. He entertains European guests sumptuously, though the entertainments are somewhat of a barbaric character, involving the cruelty of elephant and rhinoceros fights, and combats of gladiators, which sometimes prove fatal.

"Baroda," says Dr. Wilson, "is considered a cesspool of moral corruption. Notwithstanding the productions of much of its soil, it has seldom, if ever, been free from embarrassments of debt. Much caprice is shown in the exactions made from the agricultural population. The administration of justice has been most imperfect and partial." The grandeur of the *sowaris*, or processions of the Gaikwar, is quite dazzling. The prince himself rides on a noble elephant, whose howra is of silver, presented by the Queen of England; and in the procession comes the standard-bearer, also mounted on an elephant. Here to this day we see how, as Milton says:

"The gorgeous East
Showers on her kings barbaric pearl and gold."

In the neighbourhood of Gogo, north of Baroda, in the peninsula of Kathiawar, where are the best Laskars or sailors in India, is the famous Jain hill of temples called Palitana. The Jains regard temple-building as a virtue, and these temples range in date from the fifth century of our era down to the present time. The grouping together of temples is a peculiarity which the Jains practise to a greater extent than the followers of any other religion in India. The hill commands an extensive view, and the temples are among the most costly in India, built of sandstone or basalt, and neatly chunamed. The floors and doorposts are of marble, and a good deal of the workmanship is mosaic. The images are decorated with earrings, necklaces, armlets, and the wonder is that such an amount of treasure has remained unmolested. The Jaina priests here wear cloth shoes. They carry a besom to sweep the road and put all insects out of the way of harm, and a mouth-cloth to prevent insects from entering their mouths when praying. They believe that all life—the life of vegetables, brutes, men, gods—however diffused, is equally sacred. "How many lives are there," asked Dr. Wilson, "in a pound of water?" "An infinite number," was the reply. "How many are there in a bullock?" "One." "You kill then thousands of lives, while the Mussulman butcher kills one."

The city which bears the clearest marks of Mohammedan conquest in Gujarat is AHMADABAD, where there are several large mosques; but even these indicate the power of Jainism reacting upon the Moslem conquerors. A drive to the long deserted, but once lordly pleasure-place, at some distance from the city, on the banks of the river, reveals to the tourist the park-like character of Gujarat. Wheat is extensively grown, especially in the northern part, rice and the sugar-cane flourish, and mango-trees are in great abundance. Southwards cotton is widely cultivated. Along the coast there lies Somnath, where was the temple regarding which Lord Ellenborough became the laughing-stock of India when in his heated and unprincipled policy he made his empty boast that he would return with a flourish the Somnath Gates carried away by the Afghans eight centuries before. The gates never got beyond Agra; they probably never belonged to the temple, which is a ruin, now utterly forsaken, traversed by the village swine. The image in it which the Moslems destroyed was the Linga, and the remains of the temple carvings which they broke are of such a character that their destruction is scarcely a matter for surprise or regret. Farther north we reach the granite rock of GIRNAR, containing the Asoka inscriptions. On the mountain are the ruins of Buddhist dagobas, and from one of the peaks Hindus who get tired of life throw themselves down, in the hope of making a speedy journey to heaven. The view from the top embraces the adjoining hills and a wide range of low country. But the Girnar Rock ranks in historical literature with the Rosetta stone. It was first deciphered in 1835 by Dr. Wilson, who writes: "After comparing the letters with several Sanscrit alphabets in my possession, I found myself able, to my great joy and that of the Brahmans who were with me, to make out several words, and to decide as to the probable possibility of making out the whole." The inscriptions cover a hundred square feet of the uneven surface of a huge rounded and conical granite boulder twelve feet high. They record the character of the great and good Asoka.

THE GIRNAR ROCK.

Sailing still north-west along the coast of Gujarat we reach Dwarka, which was once in the west of India what Puri, the shrine of Juggernaut, is still in the east. The temple has a lofty steeple, and it stands on an elevated piece of ground with a flight of steps leading down to a creek of the sea, which is regarded as a sacred bathing-place. Its celebrity is greatly on the wane, and the decreasing number of pilgrims witnesses to the gradual decline of superstition among the people.

The state called KUTCH forms a connecting link between Gujarat and Sinde. It is almost an island, two hundred miles long by one hundred broad, intersected by two mountain ranges, and somewhat sterile in character, owing to lack of water. Cotton is the main crop. Under the influence of British counsel, specially of the excellent Dr. Gray, the Rao adopted many beneficent measures, suppressed the slave trade and infanticide, and proved himself one of the most learned and humane of the Indian princes. His capital is Bhooj, which was converted into a heap of ruins in 1819 by the great earthquake that was felt throughout India, even to Calcutta and Pondicherry. The Runn of Kutch is a flat region of seven thousand square miles, the dried-up bed of an inland sea, barren and unfruitful, and sometimes overflowed by the sea, which leaves large salt deposits. The sudden changes of land into sea, and sea into land, show the revolutions still possible on the earth.

The most northerly portion of the Bombay Presidency is SINDE, which includes the delta of the Indus. The *morale* of the policy which conquered and annexed this country in 1843 was well summed up in the parody upon

ON THE INDUS.

the short despatch of Sir C. Napier, *Peccavi*, "I have Sinde." But whatever may have been the errors of our early rule, the wise policy of Lord Dalhousie provided for such administrative and engineering improvements in Sinde, as promise to make "*young* Egypt" as it is called, more than rival *old*, although the Indus can never equal the Nile. Dr. Wilson, of Bombay, was the first Protestant missionary who opened his lips in Sinde; this was in 1850, and at Karâchi. By the battle-field of Miani and the fort of Haidarabad, where the governor had just received the homage of the chiefs, the two missionaries Duff and Wilson met thirty years ago, and made plans for educational and mission work which since have borne abundant fruit. The rising port of Karâchi has now upwards of fifty thousand inhabitants. It is connected by railway with Calcutta, by telegraph with Bassora and Europe, and by steam-ship, like Bombay, with all parts of the world.

The prosperity of India depends upon the steady growth and spread of political justice, education male and female, and Christian missions and literature. Justice must be done by the legal recognition of peasant right, making ryot and tenant joint sharers in the increasing value of the land: by reduced taxation, relieving the burdens which now crush the people; by careful curtailment of military and civil-service expenditure, moderating salaries, employing native talent; by wise expenditure in irrigation and other public works, thus averting famine and increasing the food supply; and by a steady course of firm, just, and wise legislation. In education more must be done by Government for the mass of the population, elementary schools for the people being supported, and advanced colleges for the rich being left to support themselves; while schools and colleges under missionary management are more liberally aided and encouraged, and zenana work and boarding schools for girls and orphanages supplemented by grants in aid. But, above all, our hope for India is in the circulation of the Scriptures and of a healthy Christian periodical literature, weekly and monthly, as in other parts of the world, and in the humble, zealous, self-denying labours of the "fishers of men" called and sent by the Lord Jesus, publishing the gospel of peace, bringing good tidings to the sin-burdened and sin-bound. Thus Christ's Kingdom shall prevail, and India will become hopeful, enlightened, self-governed, prosperous and free.

IN THE CHRISTIAN GIRLS' SCHOOL, AGRA.

INDEX.

LONDON: PRINTED BY WILLIAM CLOWES AND SONS, LIMITED.

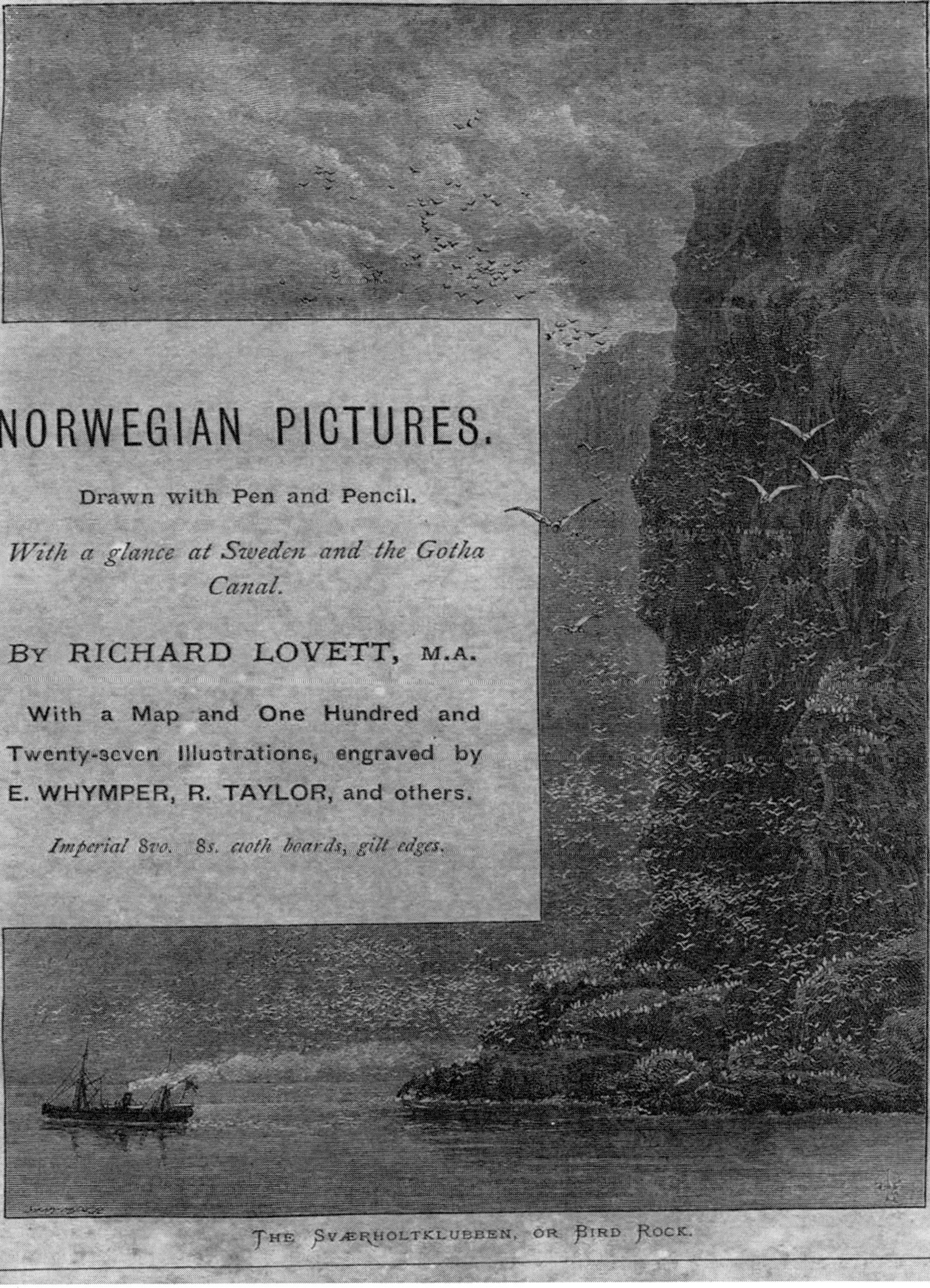

THE SVÆRHOLTKLUBBEN, OR BIRD ROCK.

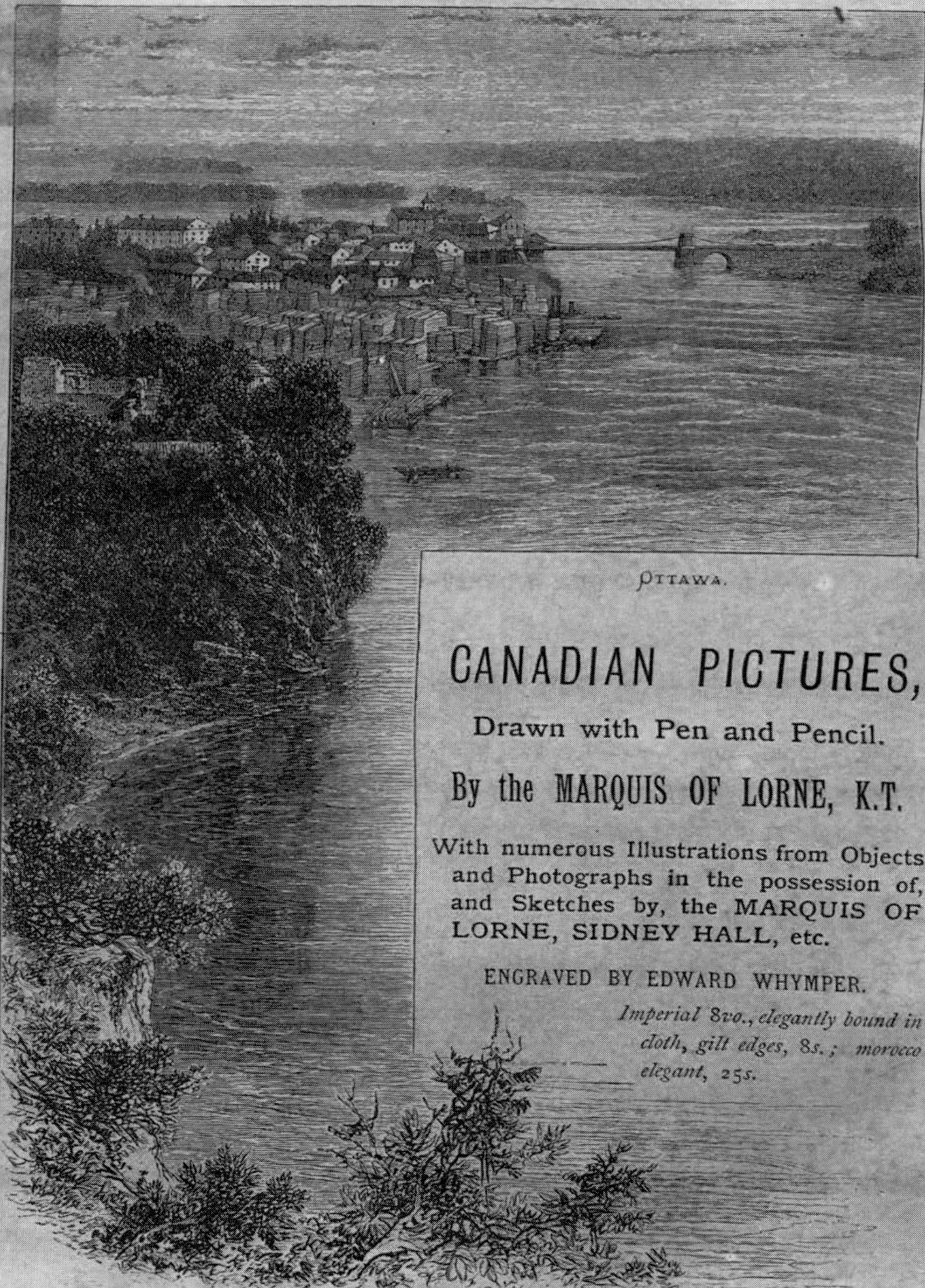

OTTAWA.

CANADIAN PICTURES,

Drawn with Pen and Pencil.

By the MARQUIS OF LORNE, K.T.

With numerous Illustrations from Objects and Photographs in the possession of, and Sketches by, the MARQUIS OF LORNE, SIDNEY HALL, etc.

ENGRAVED BY EDWARD WHYMPER.

Imperial 8vo., elegantly bound in cloth, gilt edges, 8s.; morocco elegant, 25s.

SEA PICTURES.

Drawn with Pen and Pencil. By James Macaulay, M.A., M.D., Editor of the "Leisure Hour."

Imperial 8vo., handsomely bound, gilt edges, 8s.; morocco elegant, 25s.

CLOVELLY.

UNIFORM WITH THE ABOVE IN STYLE AND PRICE.

ENGLISH PICTURES.

DRAWN WITH PEN AND PENCIL.

By the Rev. S. MANNING, LL.D., and Rev. S. G. GREEN, D.D.

With Coloured Frontispiece and Numerous Wood Engravings.

The Grampians.

SCOTTISH PICTURES.

DRAWN WITH PEN AND PENCIL.

By SAMUEL G. GREEN, D.D.

Illustrated by Eminent Artists.

Imperial 8vo., handsomely bound, gilt edges, 8s.; morocco elegant, 25s.

ON THE ERIE RAILROAD.

ST. OUEN, ROUEN.

LUTHER'S HOUSE, FRANKFURT.

FRENCH PICTURES,

DRAWN WITH PEN AND PENCIL.

By the Rev. Samuel G. Green, D.D. With upwards of 150 Fine Engravings.

Imperial 8vo., elegantly bound in cloth, gilt edges, 8s.; morocco, 25s.

PICTURES FROM THE GERMAN FATHERLAND,

Drawn with Pen and Pencil. By the Rev. Samuel G. Green, D.D. Profusely Illustrated with superior Engravings.

Bound in handsome cloth boards, full gilt, 8s.; morocco, 25s.

RUINS OF A SYNAGOGUE AT SHILOH.

THOSE HOLY FIELDS.

Palestine Illustrated by Pen and Pencil. By the Rev. Samuel Manning, LL.D.
With Numerous Fine Engravings.

COLUMNS OF TEMPLE AT LUXOR.

THE LAND OF THE PHARAOHS.

Egypt and Sinai Illustrated by Pen and Pencil. By the Rev. Samuel Manning, LL.D.
With Numerous Fine Engravings.

Imperial 8vo., elegantly bound in cloth, gilt edges, 8s.; morocco, 25s.

GOPURA AT COMBACONUM.